15-MINUTE
ITALIAN
LEARN IN JUST 12 WEEKS

FRANCESCA LOGI

DK | Penguin Random House

Senior Editors Angeles Gavira, Christine Stroyan
Project Art Editor Vanessa Marr
Jacket Design Development Manager Sophia MTT
Jacket Designer Juhi Sheth
Pre-Producer David Almond
Senior Producer Ana Vallarino
Associate Publisher Liz Wheeler
Publishing Director Jonathan Metcalf

**Language content for Dorling Kindersley by
g-and-w publishing.
Produced for Dorling Kindersley by
Schermuly Design Co.**

First American Edition, 2005
This revised edition published in the United States in 2018
by DK Publishing, 1450 Broadway,
Suite 801, New York, NY 10018

18 19 20 21 22   10 9 8 7 6 5 4 3 2
004–187955–Jan/2018

A catalog record for this book is available from the
Library of Congress.
ISBN 978-1-4654-6296-1

DK books are available at special discounts when
purchased in bulk for sales promotions, premiums, fund-
raising, or educational use. For details, contact DK
Publishing Special Markets, 1450 Broadway, Suite 801,
New York, NY 10018 or SpecialSales@dk.com

Printed in China

A WORLD OF IDEAS:
SEE ALL THERE IS TO KNOW

www.dk.com

CONTENTS

R0455960924

How to use this book

The main part of the book is devoted to 12 themed chapters, broken down into five 15-minute daily lessons, the last of which is a revision lesson. So, in just 12 weeks you will have completed the course. A concluding reference section contains a menu guide and English-to-Italian and Italian-to-English dictionaries.

Warm up
Each day starts with a warm up that encourages you to recall vocabulary or phrases you have learned previously. To the right of the heading bar you will see how long you need to spend on each exercise.

Instructions
Each exercise is numbered and introduced by instructions that explain what to do. In some cases additional information is given about the language point being covered.

Cultural/Conversational tip
These panels provide additional insights into life in Italy and language usage.

How to use the flap
The book's cover flaps allow you to conceal the Italian so that you can test whether you have remembered correctly.

Revision pages
A recap of selected elements of previous lessons helps to reinforce your knowledge.

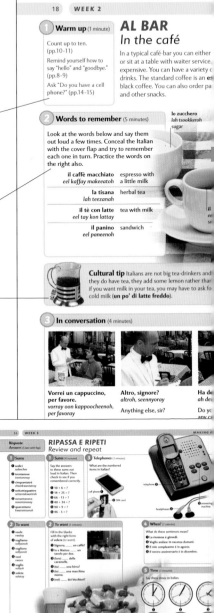

18   WEEK 2

1 Warm up (1 minute)

Count up to ten. (pp.10–11)
Remind yourself how to say "hello" and "goodbye." (pp.8–9)
Ask "Do you have a cell phone?" (pp.14–15)

AL BAR
In the café

In a typical café-bar you can either [stand] or sit at a table with waiter service [which is more] expensive. You can have a variety of [coffees and] drinks. The standard coffee is an es[presso, a small] black coffee. You can also order pa[stries] and other snacks.

2 Words to remember (5 minutes)

Look at the words below and say them out loud a few times. Conceal the Italian with the cover flap and try to remember each one in turn. Practice the words on the right also.

il caffè macchiato *eel kaffay makeeatoh*	espresso with a little milk
la tisana *lah teezanah*	herbal tea
il tè con latte *eel tay kon lattay*	tea with milk
il panino *eel paneenoh*	sandwich

lo zucchero
loh tsookkeroh
sugar

Cultural tip Italians are not big tea-drinkers and [if] they do have tea, they add some lemon rather than [milk;] if you want milk in your tea, you may have to ask fo[r] cold milk (**un po' di latte freddo**).

3 In conversation (4 minutes)

Vorrei un cappuccino, per favore.
vorray oon kappoocheenoh, per favoray

Altro, signore?
altroh, seennyoray
Anything else, sir?

Ha de[...]
ah de[...]
Do yo[u...]
any c[...]

16   WEEK 3

Risposte
Answers (Cover with flap)

RIPASSA E RIPETI
Review and repeat

1 Sums
❶ sedici
sehdeechee
❷ trentanove
trentanoveh
❸ cinquantuno
cheenkwantoonoh
❹ settantaquattro
settantakwattroh
❺ novantanove
novantanoveh
❻ quarantuno
kwarantoonoh

1 Sums (4 minutes)
Say the answers to these sums out loud in Italian. Then check to see if you remembered correctly.
❶ 10 + 6 = ?
❷ 14 + 25 = ?
❸ 66 − 13 = ?
❹ 40 + 34 = ?
❺ 90 + 9 = ?
❻ 46 − 5 = ?

3 Telephones (3 minutes)
What are the numbered items in Italian?

cell phone ❶
SIM card ❺
telephone ❷
headphones ❸
answering machine ❹

2 To want
❶ vuole
vwoley
❷ vogliamo
vollyamoh
❸ vogliono
vollyonoh
❹ vuoi
vwoee
❺ voglio
vollyoh
❻ volete
voletey

2 To want (3 minutes)
Fill in the blanks with the right form of **volere** (to want).
❶ Signora, ____ un caffè?
❷ Io e Matteo ____ un tavolo per due.
❸ (loro) ____ delle caramelle.
❹ (tu) ____ una birra?
❺ (lei) ____ una macchina nuova.
❻ (voi) ____ dei bicchieri?

4 When? (2 minutes)
What do these sentences mean?
❶ La riunione è giovedì.
❷ Voglio andare in vacanza domani.
❸ Il mio compleanno è in agosto.
❹ Il nostro anniversario è in dicembre.

5 Time (3 minutes)
Say these times in Italian.

EATING AND DRINKING 19

la brioche
lah breeosh
croissant

la crema
lah kremah
custard cream

il cappuccino
eel kappoocheenoh
coffee with frothy milk

4 Useful phrases (5 minutes)

Learn these phrases. Read the English under the pictures and say the phrase in Italian as shown on the right. Then cover up the answers on the right and test yourself.

Un caffè, per favore.
oon kaffay, per favoray

A coffee, please.

Altro?
altroh

Anything else?

Anche una brioche, per favore.
ankay oonah breeosh, per favoray

A croissant, too, please.

Quant'è?
kwantay

How much is that?

Useful phrases
Selected phrases relevant to the topic help you speak and understand.

Si, certo.
see, chertoh

Yes, certainly.

Allora, prendo una brioche. Quant'è?
allorah, prendoh oonah breeosh. kwantay

I'll have a croissant, then. How much is that?

Quattro euro, per favore.
kwattroh ayooroh, per favoray

Four euros, please.

Text styles
Distinctive text styles differentiate Italian and English, and the pronunciation guide.

In conversation
Illustrated dialogues reflecting how vocabulary and phrases are used in everyday situations appear throughout the book.

Say it
In these exercises you are asked to apply what you have learned using different vocabulary.

6 Say it (2 minutes)

Do you go to the train station?

The Vatican, please.

When's the next coach to Rome?

Dictionary
A mini-dictionary provides ready
reference from English to Italian and
Italian to English for 2,500 words.

132   DICTIONARY

DICTIONARY
English to Italian

The gender of an Italian noun is indicated by the word for the: **il** or **lo** (masculine), **la** (feminine), and their plural forms **i** or **gli** (masculine) and **le** (feminine). When **lo** or **la** are abbreviated to **l'** in front of a vowel or **h**, then the gender is indicated by the abbreviations (m) or (f). Italian adjectives (adj) vary according to the gender and number of the word they describe, and the masculine form is shown here. In general, adjectives that end in **-o** adopt an **-a** ending in the feminine form, and those that end in **-e** usually stay the same. Plural endings are **-i** for masculine and **-e** for feminine.

Menu guide
Use this guide as
a reference for
food terminology
and popular
Italian dishes.

128   MENU GUIDE

MENU GUIDE

This guide lists the most common terms you may
encounter on Italian menus or when shopping for food.
If you can't find an exact phrase, try looking up its
component parts.

Pronunciation guide

Many Italian sounds will already be familiar to you, but a few require special
attention. Take note of how these letters are pronounced:

c   an Italian **c** is pronounced *ch* before **i** or **e** but *k* before other vowels:
      cappuccino <u>k</u>appoo<u>cheenoh</u>

ch   pronounced *k* as in <u>k</u>eep

g   pronounced *j* as in <u>j</u>am before **i** or **e** but *g* as in <u>g</u>et before other vowels

gh   pronounced *g* as in <u>g</u>o

gn   pronounced *ny* like the sound in the middle of o<u>ni</u>on

gli   pronounced *ly* like the sound in the middle of mi<u>lli</u>on

h   **h** is always silent: **ho** oh (*I have*)

r   an Italian **r** is trilled like a Scottish *r*

s   an Italian **s** can be pronounced either *s* as in <u>s</u>ee or *z* as in <u>z</u>oo

sc   pronounced *sh* as in <u>sh</u>ip before **i** or **e** but *sk* as in <u>sk</u>ip before other vowels

z   an Italian **z** is pronounced *ts* as in pe<u>ts</u>

Italian vowels tend to be pronounced longer than their English equivalents,
especially:

e   as the English <u>lay</u>

i   as the English <u>keep</u>

u   as the English <u>boot</u>

After each word or phrase you will find a pronunciation transcription. Read this,
bearing in mind the tips above, and you will achieve a comprehensible result.
But remember that the transcription can only ever be an approximation and
that there is no real substitute for listening to and mimicking native speakers.

How to use the audio app

All the numbered exercises in each lesson, apart from the Warm-ups at the beginning and the Say it exercises at the end, have recorded audio, available via a free app. The app also includes a function to record yourself and listen to yourself alongside native speakers.

To start using the audio with the book, first download the **DK 15 Minute Language Course** app on your smartphone or tablet from the App Store or Google Play. Open the app and scan the QR code on the back of this book to add it to your Library. As soon as the QR code is recognized, the audio will download.

There are two ways in which you can use the audio. The first is to read through your 15-minute lessons using the book only, and then go back and work with the audio and the book together, repeating the text in the gaps provided and then recording yourself. Or you can combine the book and the audio right from the beginning, pausing the app to read the instructions on the page as you need to. Try to say the words aloud, and practice enunciating properly. Detailed instructions on how to use the app are available from the menu bar in the app.

Remember that repetition is vital to language learning. The more often you listen to a conversation or repeat an oral exercise, the more language will sink in.

Menu, Help/How to Use, Your Library

1 Getting started
The list of weeks will open when the audio has been downloaded. From here you can tap into each week's lessons.

When all the lessons in a week have been completed, the week button will be filled with color and show a check mark, so you can track your progress.

2 Lessons week by week
Each numbered exercise in a lesson is listed in the app as it appears in the book. Tap on an exercise to start.

A check mark indicates when an exercise has been completed.

3 Audio for exercises
Tap the play button to hear instructions, then the exercise. You can pause the audio at any point, and return to it.

You can tap any part of the exercise to play the audio from that point.

4 Record yourself
When you are in the *Your recordings* screen, you can record yourself reading the words or participating in the conversations with native speakers, then listen back (and rerecord if desired).

Add recording

Play recording

BUONGIORNO
Hello

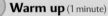

1 Warm up (1 minute)

The Warm Up panel appears at the beginning of each topic. Use it to reinforce what you have already learned and to prepare yourself for moving ahead with the new subject.

In Italy a firm handshake usually accompanies an introduction or meeting in a formal situation. Italians greet relatives and friends with a kiss on each cheek but only when they haven't met, or are not going to see each other, for a while. Men often greet each other with a hug.

Ciao!
chow
Hi!

2 Words to remember (2 minutes)

Say these polite expressions aloud. Hide the text on the left with the cover flap and try to remember the Italian for each. Check your answers and repeat, if necessary.

Buongiorno. *bwonjornoh*	Hello/Good day.
Piacere. *peeahcheray*	Pleased to meet you.
Come si chiama? *komay see keeamah*	What's your name?
Buonasera/Buonanotte. *bwonasayrah/ bwonanottay*	Good evening/ Good night.

Conversational tip Italians tend to use *sir* (**signore**), *madam* (**signora**), and *miss* (**signorina**) more than English-speakers would. These titles are also used with last names.

3 In conversation: formal (3 minutes)

Buongiorno. Mi chiamo Suzi Lee.
bwonjornoh. mee keeamoh soozee lee

Hello. My name is Suzi Lee.

Buongiorno. Marco Paoletti, piacere.
bwonjornoh. markoh pa-olettee, peeahcheray

Hello. Marco Paoletti, pleased to meet you.

Piacere.
peeahcheray

Pleased to meet you.

4 Put into practice (3 minutes)

Join in this conversation. Read the Italian beside the pictures on the left and then follow the instructions to make your reply. Then test yourself by concealing the answers with the cover flap.

Buonasera. **Buonasera signora.**
bwonasayrah *bwonasayrah seennyorah*

Good evening.

Say: Good evening madam.

Mi chiamo Marta. **Piacere.**
mee keeamoh martah *peeahcheray*

My name is Marta.

Say: Pleased to meet you.

5 Useful phrases (3 minutes)

Familiarize yourself with these phrases. Read them aloud several times and try to memorize them. Hide the Italian with the cover flap and test yourself.

Goodbye.	**Arrivederci.** *arreevederchee*
See you soon.	**A presto.** *ah prestoh*
See you tomorrow.	**A domani.** *ah domanee*
Thank you.	**Grazie.** *gratseeay*

6 In conversation: informal (3 minutes)

Allora, a domani?
allorah, ah domanee

So, see you tomorrow?

Sì, arrivederci a domani.
see, arreevederchee ah domanee

Yes, goodbye, see you tomorrow.

Arrivederci. A presto.
arreevederchee. ah prestoh

Goodbye. See you soon.

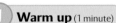

1 Warm up (1 minute)

Say "hello" and "goodbye" in Italian. (pp.8-9)

Now say "My name is... ." (pp.8-9)

Say "sir" and "madam." (pp.8-9)

I PARENTI
Relatives

In Italian the word for *the* varies depending on whether the word it refers to is masculine or feminine—for example, **il cellulare** (*cell phone*) is masculine, but **la riunione** (*meeting*) is feminine. You will sometimes find **lo** used with masculine words. **Il**, **la**, and **lo** change to **l'** before a vowel.

2 Match and repeat (5 minutes)

Look at the numbered family members in this scene and match them with the vocabulary list at the side. Read the Italian words aloud. Now, hide the list with the cover flap and test yourself.

❶ **la sorella**
   lah sorellah

❷ **il nonno**
   eel nonnoh

❸ **il padre**
   eel padray

❹ **il fratello**
   eel fratelloh

❺ **la nonna**
   lah nonnah

❻ **la figlia**
   lah feelyah

❼ **la madre**
   lah madray

❽ **il figlio**
   eel feelyoh

grandfather ❷   ❸ father

sister ❶   ❹ brother

❺ grandmother   ❻ daughter   ❼ mother   ❽ son

Conversational tip In Italian the word **nipote** means four different things: *nephew*, *niece*, *grandson*, and *granddaughter*. For *nephew* and *grandson* you use the masculine **il nipote**; for *niece* and *granddaughter* you use the feminine **la nipote**.

3 Words to remember: relatives (4 minutes)

il marito **la moglie**
eel mareetoh *lah molyay*
husband wife

Sono sposato/sposata.
sono spozatoh/spozatah
I'm married (male/female).

Look at these words and say them aloud. Hide the text on the right with the cover flap and try to remember the Italian. Check your answers and repeat, if necessary. Then practice the phrases below.

uncle	**lo zio** *loh tzeeoh*
aunt	**la zia** *lah tzeeah*
cousin	**il cugino/la cugina** *eel koojeenoh/lah koojeenah*
in-laws	**i suoceri** *ee swocheree*
I have four children.	**Ho quattro figli.** *oh kwattroh feelyee*
We have two daughters.	**Abbiamo due figlie.** *abbeeahmoh dooay feelyeeay*
I have a sister.	**Ho una sorella.** *oh oonah sorellah*
I have two brothers.	**Ho due fratelli.** *oh dooay fratellee*

4 Words to remember: numbers (5 minutes)

Memorize these words and then test yourself using the cover flap.

The word for *a* or *one* changes to match gender: **un fratello** (*a brother*, masculine); **una sorella** (*a sister*, feminine). **Un** changes to **uno** in front of **z** or **s** plus consonant: **uno zio** (*an uncle*), **uno sport** (*a sport*). **Una** changes to **un'** before a vowel: **un'amica** (*a female friend*). To make a plural, a final -a usually changes to -e: **figlia/figlie** (*daughter/daughters*). A final -o or -e usually changes to -i: **fratello/fratelli** (*brother/ brothers*). The also changes in the plural: **le** for the feminine; **i** or **gli** for the masculine.

one	**uno** *oonoh*
two	**due** *dooay*
three	**tre** *tray*
four	**quattro** *kwattroh*
five	**cinque** *cheenkway*
six	**sei** *say*
seven	**sette** *settay*
eight	**otto** *ottoh*
nine	**nove** *novay*
ten	**dieci** *deeaychee*

LA MIA FAMIGLIA
My family

1 Warm up (1 minute)

Say the Italian for as many members of the family as you can. (pp.10-11)

Say "I have two sons." (pp.10-11)

There are two ways of saying *you* in Italian: formally and informally. **Lei** is the formal version and **tu** is for family, friends, and young people. This means there are also different words for *your* (see below). It's a good idea to use the formal version until you are addressed by the other person as **tu**.

2 Words to remember (5 minutes)

There are different words for *my* and *your* in Italian, depending on whether they precede a masculine, feminine, or plural word.

mio/mia *mee-oh/me-eah*	my (masculine/ feminine singular)	
miei/mie *mee-ayee/mee-ay*	my (masculine/ feminine plural)	
tuo/tua *too-oh/too-ah*	your (informal masculine/ feminine singular)	
tuoi/tue *too-oh-ee/too-ay*	your (informal masculine/ feminine plural)	
suo/sua *soo-oh/soo-ah*	your (formal masculine/ feminine singular)	
suoi/sue *soo-oh-ee/soo-ay*	your (formal masculine/ feminine plural)	

Questi sono i miei genitori.
kwaystee sonoh ee mee-ayee jeneetoree
These are my parents.

3 In conversation (4 minutes)

Lei ha figli?
lay ah fillyee

Do you have any children?

Sì, ho due figlie.
see, oh dooay feellyay

Yes, I have two daughters.

Queste sono le mie figlie. E Lei?
kwestay sonoh lay mee-ay feellyay. ay lay

These are my daughters. And you?

Conversational tip The Italians generally ask a question by simply raising the pitch of the voice at the end of the statement: **Vuole un po' di vino?** (*Do you want a little wine?*). Some questions are introduced by a question word (*what, where, how,* and so on): **Quant'è?** (*How much is it?*), **Dove va?** (*Where are you going?*).

4 Useful phrases (3 minutes)

Read these phrases aloud several times and try to memorize them. Conceal the Italian with the cover flap and test yourself.

Do you have any brothers? (informal)	**Hai fratelli?** *ahee fratellee*
Do you have any brothers? (formal)	**Ha fratelli?** *ah fratellee*
This is my husband.	**Questo è mio marito.** *kwestoh ay mee-oh mareetoh*
This is my wife.	**Questa è mia moglie.** *kwestah ay mee-ah molyay*
Is that your sister? (informal)	**Quella è tua sorella?** *kwellah ay too-ah sorellah*
Is that your sister? (formal)	**Quella è sua sorella?** *kwellah ay soo-ah sorellah*

5 Say it (2 minutes)

Do you have any brothers and sisters? (formal)

Do you have any children? (informal)

I have two sisters.

This is my wife.

No, ma ho un nipote.
noh, mah oh oon neepotay

No, but I have a nephew.

1 **Warm up** (1 minute)

Say "See you soon."
(pp.8–9)

Say "I am married"
(pp.10–11) and "This is
my wife." (pp.12–13)

ESSERE E AVERE
To be and to have

There are some essential verbs that you can use to
make a range of useful expressions. The first of these
are **essere** (to be) and **avere** (to have). In Italian the
verb form varies according to the pronoun (I, you, he,
she, and so on). The pronoun itself is often omitted,
as it is implied by the verb.

2 **Essere: to be** (5 minutes)

Familiarize yourself with the different forms of **essere**
(to be) and, when you are confident, practice the
sentences below. Note that descriptive words can have
different endings depending on what is being described.

(io) sono *(ee-oh) sonoh*	I am
(tu) sei *(too) say*	you are (informal singular)
(Lei) è *(lay) ay*	you are (formal singular)
(lui/lei) è *(loo-ee/lay) ay*	he/she/it is
(noi) siamo *(noy) see-ahmoh*	we are
(voi) siete *(voy) see-aytay*	you are (plural)
(loro) sono *(loroh) sonoh*	they are

Sono inglese.
sonoh eenglesay
I'm English.

Di dov'è?/Di dove sei? *dee dovay/dee dovay say*	Where are you from? (formal/informal)
È contenta? *ay kontayntah*	Is she happy?
Siamo italiani. *see-ahmoh eetahleeahnee*	We're Italian.

3 Avere: to have (5 minutes)

Practice **avere** (*to have*) and the sample sentences, then test yourself.

I have	**(io) ho** *(eeoh) oh*
you have (informal singular)	**(tu) hai** *(too) ahee*
you have (formal singular)	**(Lei) ha** *(lay) ah*
he/she/it has	**(lui/lei) ha** *(loo-ee/lay) ah*
we have	**(noi) abbiamo** *(noy) abbeeahmoh*
you have (plural)	**(voi) avete** *(voy) avetay*
they have	**(loro) hanno** *(loroh) annoh*

Ha dei broccoli?
ah day brokkolee
Do you have any broccoli?

Marco has a meeting.	**Marco ha una riunione.** *markoh ah oonah reeooneeonay*
Do you have a cell phone?	**Ha un cellulare?** *ah oon chaylloolaray*
How many brothers and sisters do you have?	**Quanti fratelli ha?** *kwantee fratellee ah*

4 Negatives (4 minutes)

la bicicletta
lah beecheeklettah
bicycle

It is easy to make sentences negative in Italian. Just put **non** in front of the verb: **non siamo inglesi** (*we're not English*), **non ho fratelli** (*I don't have any brothers*).

He's not married.	**Non è sposato.** *non ay spozatoh*
I'm not sure.	**Non sono sicuro/a.** *non sonoh seekooroh/ah*
We don't have any children.	**Non abbiamo figli.** *non abbeeamoh feelyee*

Non ho l'auto.
non oh la-ootoh
I don't have a car.

RIPASSA E RIPETI
Review and repeat

Risposte
Answers (Cover with flap)

1 How many?

❶ **tre**
tray

❷ **nove**
novay

❸ **quattro**
kwattroh

❹ **due**
dooay

❺ **otto**
ottoh

❻ **dieci**
deeaychee

❼ **cinque**
cheenkway

❽ **sette**
settay

❾ **sei**
say

1 How many? (2 minutes)

Hide the answers with the cover flap. Then say the Italian numbers aloud. Check to see if you remembered the Italian correctly.

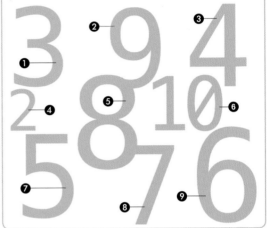

2 Hello

❶ **Buonasera, mi chiamo...**
bwonasayrah, mee keeamoh...

❷ **Piacere.**
peeahcheray

❸ **Sì sono sposato/a, e ho due figli. E Lei?**
see sonoh spozatoh/ah, ay oh dooay feelyee. ay lay

❹ **Arrivederci a domani.**
arreevederchee ah domanee

2 Hello (4 minutes)

You meet someone in a formal situation. Join in the conversation, replying in Italian following the English prompts.

Buonasera, mi chiamo Suzi.
❶ Answer the greeting and give your name.

Questo è mio marito, Piero.
❷ Say "Pleased to meet you."

Lei è sposato/a?
❸ Say "Yes, I'm married and I have two sons. And you?"

Noi abbiamo tre figlie.
❹ Say "Goodbye. See you tomorrow."

3 To have or to be (5 minutes)

Fill in the blanks with the correct form of **avere** (*to have*) or **essere** (*to be*). Check you have remembered the Italian correctly.

❶ (io) _____ sposato/a.

❷ (noi) _____ quattro figli.

❸ (lei) _____ inglese.

❹ (lei) _____ un fratello?

❺ (voi) _____ figli?

❻ (io) non _____ il cellulare

❼ (tu) _____ sicuro.

❽ (noi) _____ italiani.

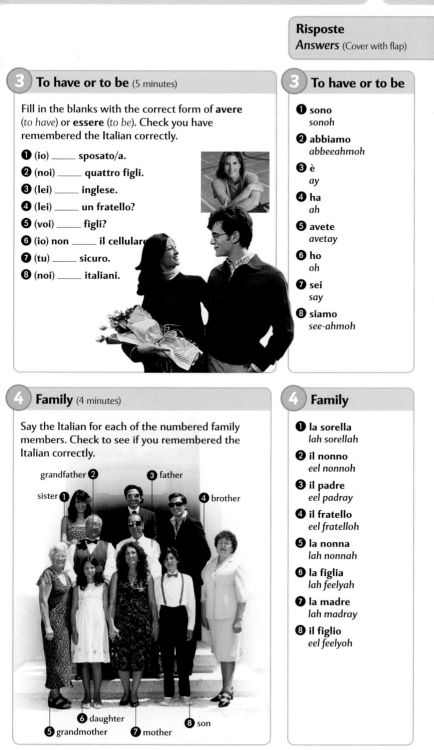

3 To have or to be

❶ **sono**
sonoh

❷ **abbiamo**
abbeeahmoh

❸ **è**
ay

❹ **ha**
ah

❺ **avete**
avetay

❻ **ho**
oh

❼ **sei**
say

❽ **siamo**
see-ahmoh

4 Family (4 minutes)

Say the Italian for each of the numbered family members. Check to see if you remembered the Italian correctly.

grandfather ❷   ❸ father

sister ❶   ❹ brother

❻ daughter   ❽ son

❺ grandmother   ❼ mother

4 Family

❶ **la sorella**
lah sorellah

❷ **il nonno**
eel nonnoh

❸ **il padre**
eel padray

❹ **il fratello**
eel fratelloh

❺ **la nonna**
lah nonnah

❻ **la figlia**
lah feelyah

❼ **la madre**
lah madray

❽ **il figlio**
eel feelyoh

1 Warm up (1 minute)

Count up to ten.
(pp.10-11)

Remind yourself how to
say "hello" and "goodbye."
(pp.8-9)

Ask "Do you have a cell
phone?" (pp.14-15)

AL BAR
In the café

In a typical café-bar you can either stand at the counter
or sit at a table with waiter service, which can be more
expensive. You can have a variety of soft or alcoholic
drinks. The standard coffee is an **espresso**, a small,
black coffee. You can also order pastries, sandwiches,
and other snacks.

2 Words to remember (5 minutes)

Look at the words below and say them
out loud a few times. Conceal the Italian
with the cover flap and try to remember
each one in turn. Practice the words on
the right also.

lo zucchero
loh tsookkeroh
sugar

il caffè macchiato *eel kaffay makeeatoh*	espresso with a little milk
la tisana *lah teezanah*	herbal tea
il tè con latte *eel tay kon lattay*	tea with milk
il panino *eel paneenoh*	sandwich

il caffè (espresso)
eel kaffay (espressoh)
small, black coffee

Cultural tip Italians are not big tea-drinkers and when
they do have tea, they add some lemon rather than milk. So
if you want milk in your tea, you may have to ask for a little
cold milk (**un po' di latte freddo**).

3 In conversation (4 minutes)

**Vorrei un cappuccino,
per favore.**
*vorray oon kappoocheenoh,
per favoray*

I'd like a cappuccino,
please.

Altro, signore?
altroh, seennyoray

Anything else, sir?

Ha delle brioche?
ah dellay breeosh

Do you have
any croissants?

la brioche
lah breeosh
croissant

la crema
lah kremah
custard cream

il cappuccino
eel kappoocheenoh
coffee with frothy milk

4 Useful phrases (5 minutes)

Learn these phrases. Read the English under the pictures and say the phrase in Italian as shown on the right. Then cover up the answers on the right and test yourself.

A coffee, please.

Un caffè, per favore.
oon kaffay, per favoray

Anything else?

Altro?
altroh

A croissant, too, please.

Anche una brioche, per favore.
ankay oonah breeosh, per favoray

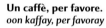

How much is that?

Quant'è?
kwantay

Sì, certo.
see, chertoh

Yes, certainly.

Allora, prendo una brioche. Quant'è?
allorah, prendoh oonah breeosh. kwantay

I'll have a croissant, then. How much is that?

Quattro euro, per favore.
kwattroh ayooroh, per favoray

Four euros, please.

AL RISTORANTE
In the restaurant

① Warm up (1 minute)

Say "I'd like." (pp.18-19)

Say "I don't have a brother." (pp.14-15)

Ask "Do you have any croissants?" (pp.18-19)

There are a variety of eating places in Italy. In a bar you can find a few snacks. A **trattoria** is a traditional restaurant with fast service. In more formal restaurants, it is often necessary to make reservations. Pizzerias are a relaxed and cheap way of dining out, and are ideal for big groups.

② Words to remember (3 minutes)

Memorize these words. Conceal the Italian with the cover flap and test yourself.

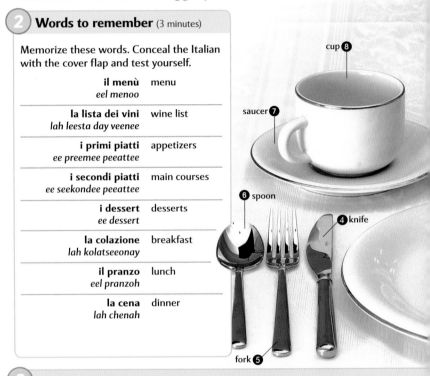

il menù *eel menoo*	menu
la lista dei vini *lah leesta day veenee*	wine list
i primi piatti *ee preemee peeattee*	appetizers
i secondi piatti *ee seekondee peeattee*	main courses
i dessert *ee dessert*	desserts
la colazione *lah kolatseeonay*	breakfast
il pranzo *eel pranzoh*	lunch
la cena *lah chenah*	dinner

cup ⑧ • saucer ⑦ • ⑥ spoon • ④ knife • fork ⑤

③ In conversation (4 minutes)

Buongiorno, ha un tavolo per quattro?
bwonjornoh, ah oon tavoloh per kwattroh

Hello. Do you have a table for four?

Ha la prenotazione?
ah lah prenotatseeonay

Do you have a reservation?

Sì, a nome Gatti.
see, anomay gattee

Yes, in the name of Gatti.

4 Match and repeat (4 minutes)

Look at the numbered items in this table setting and match them with the Italian words on the right. Read the Italian words aloud. Now, conceal the Italian with the cover flap and test yourself.

glass ❶

❷ napkin

plate ❸

❶ il bicchiere
eel beekkyayray

❷ il tovagliolo
eel tovallyohloh

❸ il piatto
eel peeattoh

❹ il coltello
eel koltelloh

❺ la forchetta
lah forkettah

❻ il cucchiaio
eel kookee-ayoh

❼ il piattino
eel peeahteenoh

❽ la tazza
lah tattsah

5 Useful phrases (3 minutes)

Practice these phrases and then test yourself using the cover flap to conceal the Italian.

What do you have for dessert?	**Cosa avete come dessert?** *kozah avaytay komay dessert*
The check, please.	**Il conto, per favore.** *eel kontoh, per favoray*

Benissimo. Che tavolo vuole?
beneesseemoh. kay tavoloh vwolay

Fine. Which table would you like?

Vicino alla finestra, per favore.
veecheenoh allah feenestrah, per favoray

Near the window, please.

Certo. Ecco.
chertoh. ekkoh

Very well. Here you are.

1 Warm up (1 minute)

What are "breakfast," "lunch," and "dinner" in Italian? (pp.20-1)

Say "I," "you" (informal), "he," "she," "we," "you" (plural), "they." (pp.14-15)

VOLERE
To want

In this section, you will learn the different forms of a verb that are essential to everyday conversation, **volere** (*to want*), including a useful polite form, **vorrei** (*I would like*). Remember to use this form when requesting something because **voglio** (*I want*) may sound too strong.

2 Volere: to want (6 minutes)

Say the different forms of **volere** (*to want*) aloud. Use the cover flap to test yourself and, when you are confident, practice the sample sentences below.

(io) voglio *vollyoh*	I want
(tu) vuoi *vwoee*	you want (informal singular)
(Lei) vuole *vwolay*	you want (formal singular)
(lui/lei) vuole *vwolay*	he/she wants
(noi) vogliamo *vollyamoh*	we want
(voi) volete *voletay*	you want (plural)
(loro) vogliono *vollyonoh*	they want

Lei vuole un'auto nuova. *lay vwolay oon a-ootoh nwovah*	She wants a new car.
Vogliamo andare in vacanza. *vollyamoh andaray een vakantsah*	We want to go on vacation.

Voglio delle caramelle.
vollyoh dellay karamayllay
I want some candy.

Conversational tip In Italian **del**, the word for *some*, changes depending on what follows, for example:
Voglio del caffè (*I want some coffee*, masculine singular)
Voglio della birra (*I want some beer*, feminine singular)
Voglio dei limoni (*I want some lemons*, masculine plural)
Voglio delle caramelle (*I want some candy*, feminine plural)
Della may be shortened to **dell'** before a vowel.

3 Polite requests (4 minutes)

There is a form of **volere** used for polite requests: (**io**) **vorrei** (*I would like*), as in **Vorrei un caffè** (*I'd like a coffee*). Practice the following sample sentences and then test yourself using the cover flap.

| I'd like a beer. | **Vorrei una birra.** |
| | *vorray oonah beerah* |

I'd like a table for tonight. | **Vorrei un tavolo per stasera.**
vorray oon tavoloh per staserah

I'd like the menu, please. | **Vorrei il menù, per favore.**
vorray eel menoo, per favoray

4 Put into practice (4 minutes)

Join in this conversation. Read the Italian beside the pictures on the left and then follow the instructions to make your reply in Italian. Test yourself by hiding the answers with the cover flap.

Buonasera. Ha la prenotazione?
bwonasayrah. ah lah prenotatseeonay

Good evening. Do you have a reservation?

Say: No, but I would like a table for three.

No, ma vorrei un tavolo per tre.
noh, mah vorray oon tavoloh per tray

Benissimo. Che tavolo vuole?
beneesseemoh. kay tavoloh vwolay

Fine. Which table would you like?

Say: Near the window please.

Vicino alla finestra, per favore.
veecheenoh allah feenestrah, per favoray

LE PIETANZE
Dishes

1 **Warm up** (1 minute)

Say "I am married" (pp.12–13) and "I'm not sure." (pp.14–15)

Ask "Do you have any brothers?" (pp.12–13)

Say "I'd like a sandwich." (pp.18-19)

Italy is famous for its cuisine and the quality of its restaurants. It also offers a wide variety of regional dishes. Pasta is a typical Italian dish, prepared in dozens of different ways. Although traditional Italian cuisine is meat-based, many restaurants now offer a vegetarian menu.

Cultural tip In many restaurants you will be able to choose a cheaper *set menu* **il menù fisso** or **il menù turistico**. *Salad* (**l'insalata**) is usually served as a *side dish* (**il contorno**).

2 **Match and repeat** (4 minutes)

Look at the numbered items and match them to the Italian words in the panel on the left.

1 **la verdura**
lah vairdoorah

2 **la frutta**
lah froottah

3 **il formaggio**
eel formajjoh

4 **la frutta secca**
la froottah sekkah

5 **la minestra**
lah meenestrah

6 **il pollo**
eel polloh

7 **il pesce**
eel peshay

8 **la pasta**
lah pastah

9 **i frutti di mare**
ee froottee dee maray

10 **la carne**
lah karnay

fruit **2**

vegetables **1**

cheese **3**

5 soup

chicken **6**

8 pasta

9 seafood

3 Words to remember: cooking methods (3 minutes)

The ending may vary depending on the gender of item described.

fried (m/f)	**fritto/a** *freettoh/ah*	
grilled	**alla griglia** *allah greellyah*	
roasted (m/f)	**arrosto** *arrostoh*	
boiled (m/f)	**lesso/a** *layssoh/ah*	
steamed	**al vapore** *al vaporay*	
rare (meat)	**al sangue** *al sangway*	

Vorrei una bistecca ben cotta.
vorray oona beestekkah ben kottah
I'd like my steak well done.

6 Say it (2 minutes)

What is **al vapore**?

I'm allergic to seafood.

I'd like a beer.

4 Words to remember: drinks (3 minutes)

Familiarize yourself with these words.

water	**l'acqua (f)** *lahkkwah*	
sparkling water	**l'acqua gassata (f)** *lahkkwah gassatah*	
still water	**l'acqua naturale (f)** *lahkkwah natooralay*	
wine	**il vino** *eel veenoh*	
beer	**la birra** *lah beerah*	
fruit juice	**il succo di frutta** *eel sookkoh dee froottah*	

nuts ❹

5 Useful phrases (2 minutes)

Practice these phrases and then test yourself.

I am a vegetarian.	**Sono vegetariano/a.** *sonoh vejetareeanoh/ah*
I am allergic to nuts.	**Sono allergico/a alla frutta secca.** *sonoh allerjeekoh/ah allah froottah sekkah*
What are **tagliatelle**?	**Cosa sono le tagliatelle?** *kozah sonoh lay tallyatellay*

fish ❼

❿ meat

RIPASSA E RIPETI
Review and repeat

1 What food?

❶ **lo zucchero**
loh tsookkeroh

❷ **la verdura**
lah vairdoorah

❸ **i frutti di mare**
ee froottee dee maray

❹ **la carne**
lah karnay

❺ **il bicchiere**
eel beekkyayray

1 What food? (4 minutes)

Name the numbered items.

❷ vegetables
sugar ❶
seafood ❸
meat ❹
glass ❺

2 This is my...

❶ **Questo è mio marito.**
kwestoh ay meeoh mareetoh

❷ **Questa è mia figlia.**
kwestah ay meeah feellyah

❸ **Queste sono le mie sorelle.**
kwestay sonoh lay meeay sorellay

2 This is my... (4 minutes)

Say these phrases in Italian.
Use **mio**, **mia**, **miei**, or **mie**.

❶ This is my husband.

❷ This is my daughter.

❸ These are my sisters.

3 I'd like...

❶ **Vorrei un caffè.**
vorray oon caffay

❷ **Vorrei un cappuccino.**
vorray oon kappoocheenoh

❸ **Vorrei una brioche.**
vorray oonah breeosh

❹ **Vorrei lo zucchero.**
vorray loh tsookkeroh

3 I'd like... (3 minutes)

Say "I'd like" the following:

croissant ❸
❹ sugar   ❶ black coffee

cappuccino ❷

1 What food?

❻ **la pasta**
lah pastah

❼ **il coltello**
eel koltelloh

❽ **il formaggio**
eel formajjoh

❾ **il tovagliolo**
eel tovallyohloh

❿ **la birra**
lah beerrah

pasta ❻
knife ❼
cheese ❽
beer ❿
napkin ❾

4 Restaurant (4 minutes)

You arrive at a restaurant. Join in the
conversation, replying in Italian where
you see the English prompts.

Buonasera.
❶ Ask "Do you have a table for one?"

Ha la prenotazione?
❷ Say "Yes, in the name of Gatti."

Benissimo.
❸ Say "I'd like the menu, please."

Vuole anche la lista dei vini?
❹ Say "No. Sparkling water, please."

Ecco.
❺ Say "I don't have a glass."

4 Restaurant

❶ **Ha un tavolo
per uno?**
*ah oon tavoloh
per oonoh*

❷ **Sì, a nome Gatti.**
see, anomay gattee

❸ **Vorrei il menù,
per favore.**
*vorray eel menoo,
per favoray*

❹ **No, acqua gassata,
per favore.**
*noh, ahkkwah
gassatah, per
favoray*

❺ **Non ho il
bicchiere.**
*non oh eel
beekkyeray*

I GIORNI E I MESI
Days and months

1 **Warm up** (1 minute)

How do you say "he is" and "they are"? (pp.14-15)

Now say "he is not" and "they are not." (pp.14-15)

What is Italian for "my mother"? (pp.10-11)

In Italian, *days of the week* (**i giorni della settimana**) and *months* (**i mesi**) do not have capital letters. Notice that with months you generally use **in**: **in ottobre** (*in October*); with days you use nothing: **lunedì** (*on Monday*), but when it means every Monday you use the article (**il/la**): **il lunedì** (*on Mondays*).

2 **Words to remember: days of the week** (5 minutes)

Familiarize yourself with these words and test yourself using the cover flap.

lunedì *loonedee*	Monday
martedì *martedee*	Tuesday
mercoledì *merkoledee*	Wednesday
giovedì *jovedee*	Thursday
venerdì *venerdee*	Friday
sabato *sabatoh*	Saturday
domenica *domeneekah*	Sunday
oggi *ojjee*	today
domani *domanee*	tomorrow
ieri *yayree*	yesterday

Ci vediamo domani.
chee vedeeamoh domanee
We meet tomorrow.

Ho una prenotazione per oggi.
oh oonah prenotatseeonay per ojjee
I have a reservation for today.

3 **Useful phrases: days** (2 minutes)

Learn these phrases and then test yourself using the cover flap.

La riunione non è martedì. *lah reeooneeonay non ay martedee*	The meeting isn't on Tuesday.
La domenica lavoro. *lah domeneekah lavoroh*	I work on Sundays.

4 Words to remember: months of the year (5 minutes)

Familiarize yourself with these words and test yourself using the cover flap.

Il nostro anniversario è in luglio.
eel nostroh anneeversareeoh
ay een loollyoh
Our anniversary is in July.

Natale è in dicembre.
natalay ay een deechembray
Christmas is in December.

January	**gennaio**	*jennaheeoh*
February	**febbraio**	*febbraheeoh*
March	**marzo**	*martsoh*
April	**aprile**	*apreelay*
May	**maggio**	*majjeeoh*
June	**giugno**	*jooneeoh*
July	**luglio**	*loollyoh*
August	**agosto**	*agostoh*
September	**settembre**	*settembray*
October	**ottobre**	*ottobray*
November	**novembre**	*novembray*
December	**dicembre**	*deechembray*
month	**mese**	*mezay*
year	**anno**	*annoh*

5 Useful phrases: months (2 minutes)

Learn these phrases and then test yourself using the cover flap.

My children are on vacation in August. **I miei bambini sono in vacanza in agosto.** *ee mee-ayee bambeenee sonoh een vakantsah een agostoh*

My birthday is in June. **Il mio compleanno è in giugno.** *eel mee-oh kompleahnnoh ay een jooneeoh*

L'ORA E I NUMERI
Time and numbers

1 Warm up (1 minute)

Count in Italian from
1 to 10. (pp.10-11)

Say "I have a reservation."
(pp.20-1)

Say "The meeting is on
Wednesday." (pp.28-9)

On a day-to-day basis Italians use the 12-hour clock, sometimes adding **di mattina** (*in the morning*), **di pomeriggio** (*in the afternoon*), **di sera** (*in the evening*), or **di notte** (*at night*). To say the time you say **Sono le...**, as in **Sono le dieci** (*It's ten o'clock*), except for *It's one o'clock*, which is **È l'una**.

2 Words to remember: time (4 minutes)

Memorize how to tell the time in Italian.

l'una *loonah*	one o'clock
l'una e cinque *loonah ay cheenkway*	five past one
l'una e un quarto *loonah ay oon kwartoh*	quarter past one
l'una e venti *loonah ay ventee*	one-twenty
l'una e mezzo *loonah ay metsoh*	one-thirty
le due meno un quarto *lay dooay menoh oon kwartoh*	quarter to two
le due meno dieci *lay dooay meno deeaychee*	ten to two

3 Useful phrases (2 minutes)

Learn these phrases and then test yourself using the cover flap.

Che ore sono? *kay oray sonoh*	What time is it?
A che ora vuole la colazione? *ah kay orah voo-olay lah kolatseeonay*	What time do you want breakfast?
Ho una prenotazione per le dodici. *oh oonah prenotatseeonay per lay dodeechee*	I have a reservation for twelve o'clock.

4 Words to remember: higher numbers (6 minutes)

To say 21, 31, and so on, you say **ventuno**, **trentuno**, etc. After that, just add the number as in **ventidue** (22), **ventitré** (23), **trentadue** (32), **trentatré** (33).

To say the date, you generally use the regular number: **Oggi è il 26 settembre** (*Today is September 26th*).

The exception is the first day of the month when you say *the first*, as in **Domani è il primo febbraio** (*Tomorrow is the first of February*).

Sono ottantacinque euro.
sonoh ottantacheenkway ayooroh
That's eighty-five euros.

eleven	**undici**	*oondeechee*
twelve	**dodici**	*dodeechee*
thirteen	**tredici**	*traydeechee*
fourteen	**quattordici**	*kwattordeechee*
fifteen	**quindici**	*kweendeechee*
sixteen	**sedici**	*sedeechee*
seventeen	**diciassette**	*deechassettay*
eighteen	**diciotto**	*deechottoh*
nineteen	**diciannove**	*deechannovay*
twenty	**venti**	*ventee*
thirty	**trenta**	*trentah*
forty	**quaranta**	*kwarantah*
fifty	**cinquanta**	*cheenkwantah*
sixty	**sessanta**	*sessantah*
seventy	**settanta**	*settantah*
eighty	**ottanta**	*ottantah*
ninety	**novanta**	*novantah*
hundred	**cento**	*chentoh*
three hundred	**trecento**	*traychentoh*
thousand	**mille**	*meellay*
ten thousand	**diecimila**	*deeaycheemeelah*
two hundred thousand	**duecentomila**	*dooaychentomeelah*
one million	**un milione**	*oon meeleeonay*

5 Say it (2 minutes)

twenty-five

sixty-eight

eighty-four

ninety-one

It's five to ten.

It's eleven-thirty.

What time is lunch?

GLI APPUNTAMENTI
Appointments

Business in Italy is still generally conducted more formally than in the United States; always address business contacts as **Lei**. Italians also tend to take a longer lunch break and, except in big cities, people often go home for their noon meal.

1 Warm up (1 minute)

Say the days of the week. (pp.28–9)

Say "It's three o'clock." (pp.30–1)

What's the Italian for "today," "tomorrow," and "yesterday"? (pp.28–9)

Benvenuto.
benvenootoh
Welcome.

la stretta di mano
lah strettah dee manoh
handshake

2 Useful phrases (5 minutes)

Learn these phrases and then test yourself.

Fissiamo un appuntamento per domani? *feesseeamoh oon appoontamentoh per domanee*	Shall we meet tomorrow?
Con chi? *kon kee*	With whom?
Quando è libero/a? *kwandoh ay leeberoh/ah*	When are you free?
Mi dispiace, sono impegnato/a. *mee deespeeachay, sonoh eempennyatoh/ah*	I'm sorry, I am busy.
Va bene giovedì? *vah benay jovedee*	How about Thursday?
Per me va bene. *per may vah benay*	That's good for me.

3 In conversation (4 minutes)

Buongiorno. Ho un appuntamento.
bwonjornoh. oh oon appoontamentoh

Hello. I have an appointment.

Con chi?
kon kee

With whom?

Con il signor Baroni.
kon eel seennyor baronee

With Mr. Baroni.

4 Put into practice (5 minutes)

Practice these phrases. Then cover the text on the right and say the answering part of the dialogue in Italian. Check your answers and repeat if necessary.

Fissiamo un appuntamento per giovedì?
feesseeamoh oon appoontamentoh per jovedee

Shall we meet on Thursday?

Say: Sorry, I'm busy.

Mi dispiace, giovedì sono impegnato.
mee deespeeachay, jovedee sonoh eempennyatoh

Quando è libero?
kwandoh ay liberoh

When are you free?

Say: Tuesday afternoon.

Martedì pomeriggio.
martedee pomereejjoh

Per me va bene.
per may vah benay

That's good for me.

Ask: At what time?

A che ora?
ah kay orah

Alle quattro, se per Lei va bene.
allay kwattroh, say per lay vah benay

At four o'clock, if that's good for you.

Say: It's good for me.

Per me va bene.
per may vah benay

Benissimo, a che ora?
beneesseemoh, ah kay orah

OK, at what time?

Alle tre, ma sono un po' in ritardo.
allay tray, mah sonoh oon poh een reetardoh

At three o'clock, but I'm a little late.

Non si preoccupi. Prego, si accomodi.
non see prayokkoopee. pregoh, see akkomodee

Don't worry. Take a seat, please.

1 **Warm up** (1 minute)

How do you say "I'm sorry"? (pp.32-3)

Say "I'd like an appointment." (pp.32-3)

How do you say "with whom?" in Italian? (pp.32-3)

AL TELEFONO
On the telephone

In Italy you always dial the *full area code* (**il prefisso**) and the number. The emergency number for *police* (**Carabinieri**), *ambulance* (**l'ambulanza**), or *fire services* (**i vigili del fuoco**) is 112.

2 **Match and repeat** (4 minutes)

Match the numbered items to the Italian in the panel on the left and test yourself.

1 **il caricabatterie**
eel karikabatereeay

2 **il telefono**
eel telayfonoh

3 **la segreteria telefonica**
la segretereeah telayfoneekah

4 **gli auricolari**
lly awreekolaree

5 **il cellulare**
eel chelloolaray

6 **la carta SIM**
la karta seem

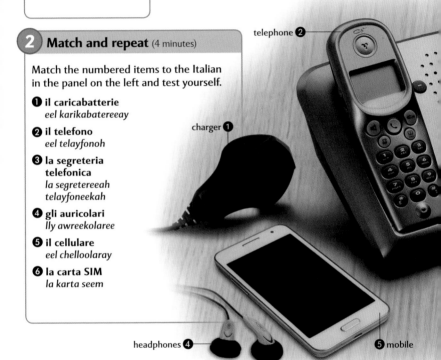

telephone **2**

charger **1**

headphones **4**

5 mobile

3 **In conversation** (4 minutes)

Pronto? Bonanni.
prontoh? bonannee

Hello? Bonanni's.

Buongiorno. Vorrei parlare con il dottor Pieri.
bwonjornoh. vorray parlaray kon eel dottor pyayree

Hello. I'd like to speak to Dr. Pieri.

Chi parla?
kee parlah

Who's speaking?

SIM card **6**

Vorrei comprare una carta SIM.
vorray kompraray oonah karta SIM
I'd like to buy a SIM card.

3 answering machine

4 Useful phrases (4 minutes)

Practice these phrases. Then test yourself using the cover flap.

I'd like the number for Mario.

Posso avere il numero di Mario?
possoh averay eel noomayroh dee mareeoh

I'd like to speak to Federico Martini.

Vorrei parlare con Federico Martini.
vorray parlaray kon fedayreekoh marteenee

Can I leave a message?

Posso lasciare un messaggio?
possoh lasharay oon messajjoh

Sorry, I have the wrong number.

Scusi, ho sbagliato numero.
skoozee, oh sballyatoh noomayroh

5 Say it (2 minutes)

I'd like to speak to Mr. Hachart.

Can I leave a message for Emma?

Luciano Salvetti, della tipografia Bartoli.
loochanoh salvettee, della teepografeeah bartolee

Luciano Salvetti of Bartoli Printers.

Mi dispiace, la linea è occupata.
mee deespeeachay, lah leeneah ay okkoopatah

I'm sorry. The line is busy.

Può farmi richiamare, per favore?
puoh farmee reekeeamaray, per favoray

Can he call me back, please?

RIPASSA E RIPETI
Review and repeat

1 Sums

❶ **sedici**
sedeechee

❷ **trentanove**
trentanovay

❸ **cinquantatré**
cheenkwantatray

❹ **settantaquattro**
settantakwattroh

❺ **novantanove**
novantanovay

❻ **quarantuno**
kwarantoonoh

1 Sums (4 minutes)

Say the answers
to these sums out
loud in Italian. Then
check to see if you
remembered correctly.

❶ $10 + 6 = ?$
❷ $14 + 25 = ?$
❸ $66 - 13 = ?$
❹ $40 + 34 = ?$
❺ $90 + 9 = ?$
❻ $46 - 5 = ?$

3 Telephones (3 minutes)

What are the numbered
items in Italian?

cell phone ❶

❷ SIM card

2 To want

❶ **vuole**
vwolay

❷ **vogliamo**
vollyamoh

❸ **vogliono**
vollyonoh

❹ **vuoi**
vwoee

❺ **voglio**
vollyoh

❻ **volete**
voletay

2 To want (3 minutes)

Fill in the blanks
with the right form
of **volere** (to want).

❶ Signora, _____ un caffè?
❷ Io e Matteo _____ un
tavolo per due.
❸ (loro) _____ delle
caramelle.
❹ (tu) _____ una birra?
❺ (io) _____ una macchina
nuova.
❻ (voi) _____ dei bicchieri?

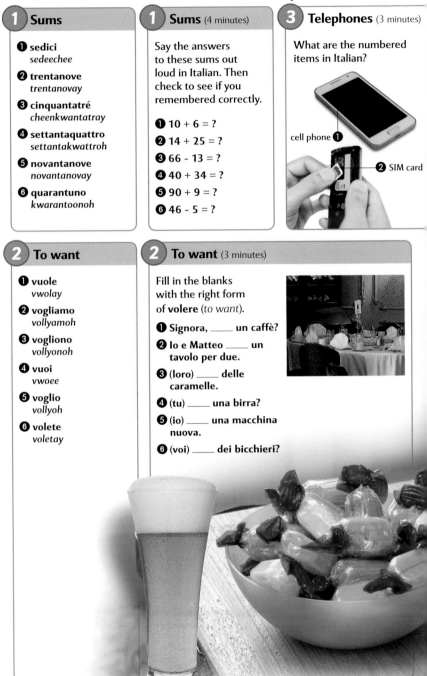

3 Telephones

❶ il cellulare
eel chelloolaray

❷ la carta SIM
la karta seem

❸ il telefono
eel telayfonoh

❹ gli auricolari
lly awreekolaree

❺ la segreteria telefonica
la segretereeah telayfoneekah

telephone ❸

answering ❺ machine

headphones ❹

4 When? (2 minutes)

What do these sentences mean?

❶ La riunione è giovedì.

❷ Voglio andare in vacanza domani.

❸ Il mio compleanno è in agosto.

❹ Il nostro anniversario è in dicembre.

4 When?

❶ The meeting is on Thursday.

❷ I want to go on vacation tomorrow.

❸ My birthday is in August.

❹ Our anniversary is in December.

5 Time (3 minutes)

Say these times in Italian.

❶ ❷ ❸

❹ ❺ ❻

5 Time

❶ l'una
loonah

❷ l'una e cinque
loonah ay cheenkway

❸ l'una e venti
loonah ay ventee

❹ l'una e mezzo
loonah ay metsoh

❺ l'una e un quarto
loonah ay oon kwartoh

❻ le due meno dieci
lay dooay menoh deeaychee

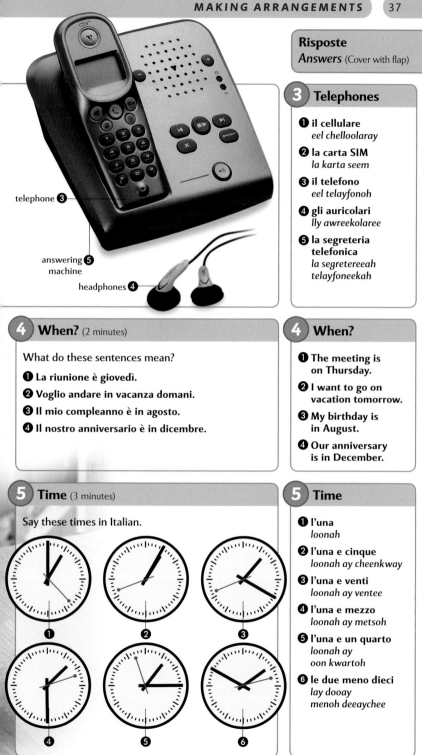

1 Warm up (1 minute)

Count to 100 in tens.
(pp.10-11 and pp.30-1)

Ask "At what time?"
(pp.30-1)

Say "half-past one."
(pp.30-1)

ALLA BIGLIETTERIA
At the ticket office

In Italy you must be sure to *validate* (**convalidare**) your ticket before getting on the train by stamping it in one of the special small yellow machines installed in every train station for this purpose. Fines are imposed on travelers who have forgotten to validate their tickets.

2 Words to remember (3 minutes)

Learn these words and then test yourself.

la stazione *lah statseeonay*	station
il treno *eel trenoh*	train
la prenotazione *la prenotatseeonay*	reservation
il biglietto *eel beellyettoh*	ticket
sola andata *solah andatah*	one-way
andata e ritorno *andatah ay reetornoh*	round-trip
prima/seconda classe *preemah/sekondah klassay*	first/second class
la coincidenza *la koeencheedentsa*	connection

il passeggero
eel passejjayroh
passenger

il cartello
eel kartelloh
sign

La stazione è affollata.
lah statseeonay ay affollahtah
The station is crowded.

3 In conversation (4 minutes)

Due biglietti per Roma, per favore.
dooay beellyettee per rohmah, per favoray

Two tickets to Rome, please.

Andata e ritorno?
andatah ay reetornoh

Round-trip?

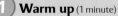

Sì. C'è la prenotazione obbligatoria?
see. chay lah prenotatseeonay obbleegatoryah

Yes. Do I need to reserve seats?

4 Useful phrases (5 minutes)

Learn these phrases and then test yourself using the cover flap.

Il treno per Firenze è in ritardo.
eel trenoh per firentsay ay een reetardoh
The train to Florence is late.

il binario
eel beenareeoh
platform

How much is a ticket to Genoa?	**Quanto costa un biglietto per Genova?** *kwantoh kostah oon beellyettoh per jenovah*
Do you take credit cards?	**Accettate la carta di credito?** *acchettatay lah kartah dee kredeetoh*
Do I have to change trains?	**Devo cambiare?** *devoh kambeearay*
Which platform does the train leave from?	**Da quale binario parte il treno?** *dah kwalay beenareeoh partay eel trenoh*
Are there discounts?	**Ci sono delle riduzioni?** *chee sonoh dellay reedootseeonee*
What time does the train to Naples leave?	**A che ora parte il treno per Napoli?** *ah kay orah partay eel trenoh per napolee*

5 Say it (2 minutes)

Which platform does the train to Genoa leave from?

Three return tickets to Naples, please.

Cultural tip Most train stations have *automatic ticket machines* (**la biglietteria automatica**), which accept credit and debit cards as well as cash.

No. Sono quaranta euro.
noh. sonoh kwarantah ayooroh

No. It's forty euros.

Accettate la carta di credito?
acchettatay lah kartah dee kredeetoh

Do you take credit cards?

Certo. Il treno parte dal binario uno.
chertoh. eel trenoh partay dal beenareeoh oonoh

Certainly. The train leaves from platform one.

ANDARE E PRENDERE
To go and to take

1 **Warm up** (1 minute)

How do you say "train"? (pp.38-9)

What does "Da quale binario parte il treno?" mean? (pp.38-9)

Ask "When are you free?" (pp.32-3)

Andare (to go) and **prendere** (to take) are essential verbs in Italian that you will need to use frequently in everyday conversation as you find your way around. You can also use **prendere** when you talk about food and drink—for example, to say **prendo un caffè** (I'll have a coffee).

2 **Andare: to go** (6 minutes)

Say the different forms of **andare** (to go) aloud. Use the cover flaps to test yourself and, when you are confident, practice the sample sentences below.

(io) vado *(eeoh) vadoh*	I go
(tu) vai *(too) vaee*	you go (informal singular)
(Lei) va *(lay) vah*	you go (formal singular)
(lui/lei) va *(looee/lay) vah*	he/she/it goes
(noi) andiamo *(noy) andeeamoh*	we go
(voi) andate *(voy) andatay*	you go (plural)
(loro) vanno *(loroh) vannoh*	they go
Dove va, signora? *dovay vah, seennyorah*	Where are you going, madam?
Vorrei andare in treno. *vorray andaray een trenoh*	I'd like to go by train.

Vado a Pisa.
vadoh ah peesah
I am going to Pisa.

Conversational tip In Italian the present tense includes a sense of continuous action. You use the same verb form to say *I go* and *I am going*. **Vado a Roma** means both *I am going to Rome* and *I go to Rome*. The same is true of other verbs; for example, **prendo il taxi** means *I am taking the taxi* and *I take the taxi*.

3 Prendere: to take (6 minutes)

Say the different forms of **prendere** (*to take*) aloud and test yourself.

(io) prendo *(eeoh) prendoh*	I take
(tu) prendi *(too) prendee*	you take (informal)
(Lei) prende *(lay) prenday*	you take (formal)
(lui/lei) prende *(looee/lay) prenday*	he/she/it takes
(noi) prendiamo *(noy) prendeeamoh*	we take
(voi) prendete *(voy) prendetay*	you take (plural)
(loro) prendono *(loroh) prendonoh*	they take

Prendo la metro tutti i giorni.
prendoh lah metroh toottee ee jornee
I take the metro every day.

Non voglio prendere un taxi. *non vollyoh prenderay oon taxee*	I don't want to take a taxi.
Prenda la prima a sinistra. *prenda lah preemah ah seeneestrah*	Take the first left.
Lui prende il vitello. *looee prenday eel veetelloh*	He'll have the veal.

4 Put into practice (2 minutes)

Cover the text on the right and complete the dialogue in Italian.

Dove va? *dovay vah*	**Vado alla stazione.** *vadoh allah statseeonay*
Where are you going?	
Say: I'm going to the station.	
Vuole prendere la metro? *vwolay prenderay lah metroh*	**No, voglio andare in autobus.** *noh, vollyoh andaray een a-ootoboos*
Do you want to take the metro?	
Say: No, I want to go by bus.	

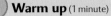

1 Warm up (1 minute)

Say "I'd like to go to the station." (pp.40-1)

Ask "Where are you going?" (pp.40-1)

Say "fruit" and "cheese." (pp.24-5)

TAXI, AUTOBUS, E METRO
Taxi, bus, and metro

In Italy you generally don't hail taxis, but go to a taxi stand. You can buy bus tickets at a newsstand and then validate them in the machine on the bus. You can use the same tickets both on the buses and on the metro.

2 Words to remember (4 minutes)

Familiarize yourself with these words.

l'autobus (m) *la-ootoboos*	bus (local)
il pullman *eel poolman*	bus (long-distance)
la stazione dei pullman/ della metro *lah statseeonay day poolman/dellah metroh*	bus/metro station
la fermata dell'autobus *lah fermatah della-ootoboos*	bus stop
il biglietto *eel beellyettoh*	fare
il posteggio dei taxi *eel postejjoh day taxee*	taxi stand

Passa di qui il quarantasei?
passah dee kwee eel kwarantasay
Does the Route 46 bus stop here?

3 In conversation: taxi (2 minutes)

Al mercato di San Lorenzo, per favore.
al merkatoh dee san lorentsoh, per favoray

To the San Lorenzo market, please.

Benissimo, signore.
beneesseemoh, seennyoray

Very well, sir.

Mi lasci qui, per favore.
mee lashee kwee, per favoray

Can you drop me here, please?

4 Useful phrases (4 minutes)

Learn these phrases and then test yourself using the cover flap.

I'd like a taxi to go to the Colosseum.	**Vorrei un taxi per andare al Colosseo.** *vorray oon taxee per andaray al kolossayoh*
When is the next bus to the Capitol?	**Quando passa il prossimo autobus per il Campidoglio?** *kwandoh passah eel prosseemoh a-ootoboos per eel kampeedollyoh*
How do you get to the Vatican?	**Scusi, per andare al Vaticano?** *skoozee, per andaray al vateekahnoh*
Please wait for me.	**Mi aspetti, per favore.** *mee aspettee, per favoray*

Cultural tip In Italy the metro exists only in Milan, Rome, and Naples. There are only a few lines and they are identified by numbers (M1, M2, M3 in Milan) or letters of the alphabet (MA, MB in Rome). Look for the relevant end station to find the direction you need.

6 Say it (2 minutes)

Do you go to the train station?

The Vatican, please.

When's the next coach to Rome?

5 In conversation: bus (2 minutes)

Scusi, va al museo?
skoozee, vah al moozayoh

Do you go to the museum?

Sì. Non è lontano.
see. non ay lontanoh

Yes. It's not very far.

Può dirmi quando devo scendere?
pwoh deermee kwandoh devoh shenderay

Can you tell me when to get off?

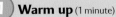

1 Warm up (1 minute)

How do you say "I have..."? (pp.14-15)

Say "my father," "my sister," and "my parents." (pp.12-13)

Say "I'm going to Rome." (pp.40-1)

IN AUTO
On the road

Be sure to familiarize yourself with the Italian rules of the road before driving in Italy. Italian **autostrade** (*expressways*) are fast but expensive *toll* (**il pedaggio**) roads. You usually take a ticket as you enter the expressway and pay according to the distance traveled as you leave it.

2 Match and repeat (4 minutes)

Match the numbered items to the list on the left, then test yourself.

❶ il bagagliaio
eel bagallyaeeoh

❷ il parabrezza
eel parabretsah

❸ il cofano
eel kofanoh

❹ la ruota
lah rwotah

❺ la gomma
lah gommah

❻ lo sportello
loh sportelloh

❼ il paraurti
eel parahoortee

❽ i fari
ee faree

❶ trunk

wheel ❹

tire ❺

door ❻

Cultural tip In Italy many gas stations still have a pump attendant, and many are closed for lunch. Sometimes you can serve yourself and pay a cheaper rate.

3 Road signs (2 minutes)

Senso unico
senso uneekoh

One way

Rotatoria
rotatoreeah

Roundabout

Dare la precedenza
daray lah prechedentsah

Yield

4 Useful phrases (4 minutes)

Learn these phrases and then test yourself using the cover flap.

My turn signal doesn't work.	**La freccia non funziona.** *lah frechah non foontseeonah*
Fill it up, please.	**Il pieno, per favore.** *eel pyaynoh, per favoray*

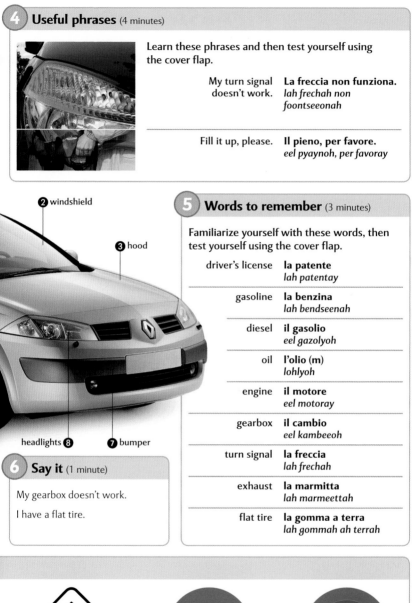

❷ windshield

❸ hood

headlights ❽ ❼ bumper

5 Words to remember (3 minutes)

Familiarize yourself with these words, then test yourself using the cover flap.

driver's license	**la patente** *lah patentay*
gasoline	**la benzina** *lah bendseenah*
diesel	**il gasolio** *eel gazolyoh*
oil	**l'olio (m)** *lohlyoh*
engine	**il motore** *eel motoray*
gearbox	**il cambio** *eel kambeeoh*
turn signal	**la freccia** *lah frechah*
exhaust	**la marmitta** *lah marmeettah*
flat tire	**la gomma a terra** *lah gommah ah terrah*

6 Say it (1 minute)

My gearbox doesn't work.

I have a flat tire.

Diritto di precedenza
deereettoh dee prechedentsah

Priority road

Divieto di accesso
deevyaytoh dee acchessoh

Do not enter

Sosta vietata
sostah veeaytatah

No parking

RIPASSA E RIPETI
Review and repeat

1 Transport

❶ l'autobus
la-ootoboos

❷ il taxi
eel taxee

❸ l'auto
la-ootoh

❹ la bicicletta
lah beecheeklettah

❺ la metro
lah metroh

1 Transport (3 minutes)

Name these forms of transportation in Italian.

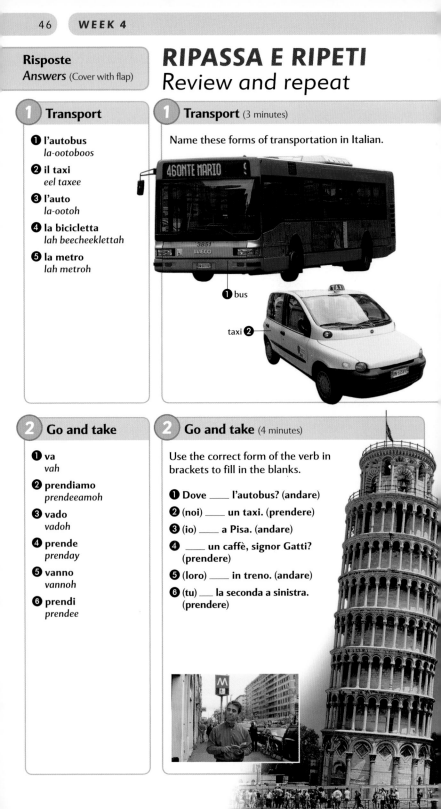

❶ bus

taxi ❷

2 Go and take

❶ va
vah

❷ prendiamo
prendeeamoh

❸ vado
vadoh

❹ prende
prenday

❺ vanno
vannoh

❻ prendi
prendee

2 Go and take (4 minutes)

Use the correct form of the verb in brackets to fill in the blanks.

❶ Dove ____ l'autobus? (andare)

❷ (noi) ____ un taxi. (prendere)

❸ (io) ____ a Pisa. (andare)

❹ ____ un caffè, signor Gatti? (prendere)

❺ (loro) ____ in treno. (andare)

❻ (tu) ____ la seconda a sinistra. (prendere)

3 Lei or tu?
(4 minutes)

Use the correct form of *you*.

❶ You are in a café. Ask "Do you have croissants?"

❷ You are with a friend. Ask "Do you want a beer?"

❸ You are talking to a business contact. Ask "Do you have an appointment?"

❹ You are on the bus. Ask "Do you go to the station?"

❺ Ask your friend where she's going tomorrow.

❻ Ask your (female) client "Are you free on Wednesday?"

3 Lei or tu?

❶ **Ha delle brioche?**
ah dellay breeosh

❷ **Vuoi una birra?**
vwoee oonah beerah

❸ **Ha un appuntamento?**
ah oon appoontamentoh

❹ **Va alla stazione?**
vah allah statseeonay

❺ **Dove vai domani?**
dovay vaee domanee

❻ **È libera mercoledì?**
ay leeberah merkoledee

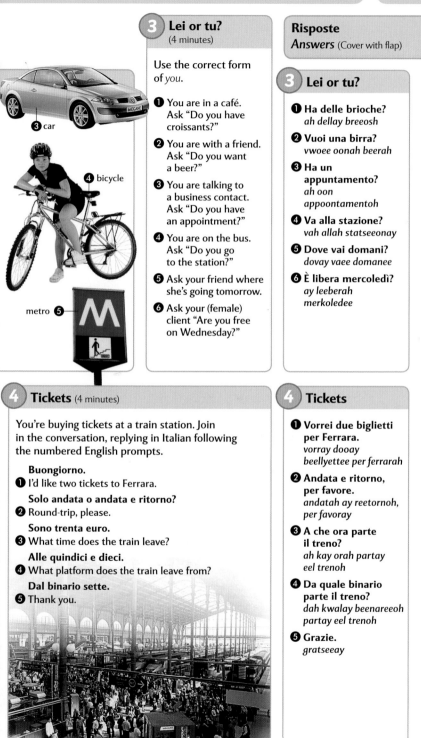

③ car

④ bicycle

metro **⑤**

4 Tickets (4 minutes)

You're buying tickets at a train station. Join in the conversation, replying in Italian following the numbered English prompts.

Buongiorno.
❶ I'd like two tickets to Ferrara.

Solo andata o andata e ritorno?
❷ Round-trip, please.

Sono trenta euro.
❸ What time does the train leave?

Alle quindici e dieci.
❹ What platform does the train leave from?

Dal binario sette.
❺ Thank you.

4 Tickets

❶ **Vorrei due biglietti per Ferrara.**
vorray dooay beellyettee per ferrarah

❷ **Andata e ritorno, per favore.**
andatah ay reetornoh, per favoray

❸ **A che ora parte il treno?**
ah kay orah partay eel trenoh

❹ **Da quale binario parte il treno?**
dah kwalay beenareeoh partay eel trenoh

❺ **Grazie.**
gratseeay

1 Warm up (1 minute)

Ask "How do you get to the museum?" (pp.42-3)

Say "I want to take the metro" and "I don't want to take a taxi." (pp.40-1)

IN CITTÀ
Around town

Most Italian towns (**la città**) and larger villages (**il paese**) still have a market day for fresh produce and a thriving local community of small shops and businesses. There may be parking restrictions in the downtown area. In Rome, parking in the central **zona tutelata** is prohibited on weekdays.

2 Match and repeat (4 minutes)

Match the numbered locations to the words in the panel.

❶ il municipio
eel mooneecheepeeoh

❷ la chiesa
lah keeayzah

❸ il ponte
eel pontay

❹ il centro città
eel chentroh cheettah

❺ il parcheggio
eel parkejjoh

❻ la piazza
lah peeatsah

❼ il museo
eel moozayoh

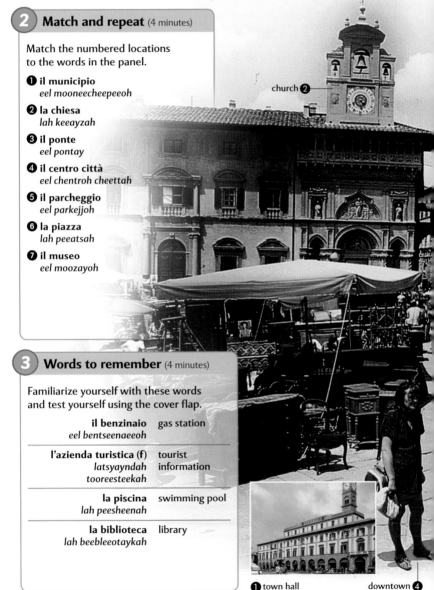

church ❷

3 Words to remember (4 minutes)

Familiarize yourself with these words and test yourself using the cover flap.

il benzinaio *eel bentseenaeeoh*	gas station
l'azienda turistica (f) *latsyayndah tooreesteekah*	tourist information
la piscina *lah peesheenah*	swimming pool
la biblioteca *lah beebleeotaykah*	library

❶ town hall   downtown ❹

4 Useful phrases (4 minutes)

Il duomo è in centro.
eel dwomoh ay een chentroh
The cathedral is downtown.

Learn these phrases and then test yourself using the cover flap.

Is there an art gallery in town?	**C'è una pinacoteca in città?** *chay oonah peenacotekah een cheettah*
Is it far from here?	**È lontano da qui?** *ay lontanoh da kwee*
There is a swimming pool near the bridge.	**C'è una piscina vicino al ponte.** *chay oonah peesheenah veecheenoh al pontay*
There isn't a library.	**Non c'è una biblioteca.** *non chay oonah beebleeotaykah*

5 Put into practice (2 minutes)

Join in this conversation. Read the Italian on the left and follow the instructions to make your reply. Then test yourself by concealing the answers with the cover flap.

bridge ❸

parking lot ❺

square ❻

Dica? *deekah* Can I help you? Ask: Is there a library in town?	**C'è una biblioteca in città?** *chay oonah beebleeotaykah een cheettah*
No, ma c'è un museo. *noh, mah chay oon moozayoh* No, but there's a museum. Ask: How do I get to the museum?	**E per andare al museo?** *ay per andaray al moozayoh*
È nella piazza. *ay nellah peeatsah* It's in the square. Say: Thank you.	**Grazie.** *gratseeay*

museum ❼

LE INDICAZIONI
Finding your way

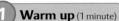

1 Warm up (1 minute)

How do you say "to the station"? (pp.40-1)

Say "Take the first left." (pp.40-1)

Ask "Where are you going?" (pp.40-1)

You'll often find a *town map* (**pianta della città**) situated around town, usually near the town hall or tourist office. In the older parts of Italian towns there are often narrow streets in which you will usually find a one-way system in operation. Parking is usually restricted.

2 Useful phrases (4 minutes)

Practice these phrases and then test yourself.

Giri a sinistra/destra. *jeeree ah seeneestrah/destrah*	turn left/right
A sinistra/destra. *ah seeneestrah/destrah*	on the left/right
Sempre dritto. *sempray dreettoh*	straight ahead
Per andare alla piscina? *per andaray allah peesheenah*	How do I get to the swimming pool?
La prima a sinistra. *ah preemah ah seeneestrah*	first left
La seconda a destra. *lah sekondah ah destrah*	second right

il municipio
eel mooneecheepeeoh
town hall

la zona pedonale
lah tsonah pedonalay
pedestrian zone

Alla piazza giri a sinistra.
allah peeatsah jeeree ah seeneestrah
At the square, turn left.

3 In conversation (4 minutes)

C'è un ristorante in città?
chay oon reestorantay een cheettah

Is there a restaurant in town?

Sì, vicino alla stazione.
see, veecheenoh allah statseeonay

Yes, near the station.

E per andare alla stazione?
ay per andaray allah statseeonay

How do I get to the station?

4 Words to remember (4 minutes)

Mi sono persa.
mee sonoh persah
I'm lost.

Familiarize yourself with these words and test yourself using the cover flap.

traffic lights	**il semaforo** *eel semaforoh*
corner	**l'angolo (m)** *langoloh*
street/road	**la strada** *lah stradah*
intersection	**l'incrocio (m)** *leenkrochoh*
map	**la pianta** *lah peeantah*
overpass	**il cavalcavia** *eel kavalkaveeah*
across from	**davanti a** *davantee ah*
at the end of the street	**in fondo alla strada** *een fondoh allah stradah*

il monumento
eel monoomentoh
monument

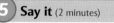

Dove siamo?
dovay seeahmoh
Where are we?

5 Say it (2 minutes)

Turn right at the end of the street.

It's across from the town hall.

It's ten minutes by bus.

Al semaforo giri a sinistra.
al semaforoh jeeree ah seeneestrah

Turn left at the traffic lights.

È lontano?
ay lontanoh

Is it far?

No, cinque minuti a piedi.
noh, cheenkway meenootee ah peeaydee

No, it's five minutes on foot.

1 **Warm up** (1 minute)

Say the days of the week in Italian. (pp.28–9)

How do you say "At six o'clock"? (pp.30–1)

Ask "What time is it?" (pp.30–1)

IL TURISMO
Sightseeing

Most national museums close on Mondays; a few are open on some public holidays. Many stores close for lunch, especially in small towns, and public buildings and banks are generally closed in the afternoon. Stores often close on Sundays, except in some tourist areas.

2 **Words to remember** (4 minutes)

Familiarize yourself with these words and test yourself using the cover flap.

la guida *lah gweedah*	guidebook
la tariffa ridotta *lah tareefah reedottah*	discount rate
l'orario di apertura (m) *lorareeoh dee apertoorah*	opening times
il giorno festivo *eel jornoh festeevoh*	public holiday
l'entrata libera *lentratah leebayrah*	free admission

la visita guidata
lah veeseetah gweedatah
guided tour

Cultural tip You will be asked to pay an admission fee in most museums, historic buildings, and even some churches. *Children* (**bambini**), *students* (**studenti**), or *pensioners* (**pensionati**) can ask for the discount rate, which is sometimes available.

3 **In conversation** (3 minutes)

È aperto oggi pomeriggio?
ay apertoh ojjee pomereejjoh

Are you open this afternoon?

Sì, ma chiudiamo alle sei.
see, mah kyoodeeamoh allay say

Yes, but we close at six o'clock.

C'è l'accesso per i disabili?
chay lacchayssoh per ee deezabeelee

Do you have access for the disabled?

4 Useful phrases (3 minutes)

Learn these phrases and then test yourself using the cover flap.

What time do you open/close?	**A che ora aprite/chiudete?** *ah kay orah apreetay/ keeoodetay*
Where are the restrooms?	**Dov'è la toilette?** *dovay lah toyeeletay*
Is there access for the disabled?	**C'è l'accesso per i disabili?** *chay lacchayssoh per ee deezabeelee*

5 Put into practice (4 minutes)

Cover the text on the right and complete the dialogue in Italian.

Spiacente. Il museo è chiuso. *speeachentay. eel moozayoh ay keeoozoh*

Sorry. The museum is closed.

Ask: Are you open on Mondays?

È aperto il lunedì? *ay apertoh eel loonedee*

Sì, ma chiude presto. *see, mah keeooday prestoh*

Yes, but we close early.

Ask: What time?

A che ora? *ah kay orah*

Sì, là c'è l'ascensore. *see, lah chay lashaynsoray*

Yes, there's an elevator over there.

Grazie. Vorrei quattro biglietti. *gratseeay. vorray kwattroh beellyettee*

Thank you. I'd like four admission tickets.

Ecco a lei. La guida è gratuita. *ekkoh ah lay. lah gweedah ay gratweetah*

Here you are. The guidebook is free.

1 Warm up (1 minute)

Say "You're on time." (pp.14-15)

What's the Italian for "ticket"? (pp.38-9)

Say "I am going to New York." (pp.40-1)

ALL'AEROPORTO
At the airport

Although the airport environment is largely universal, it is sometimes useful to be able to understand key words and phrases in Italian. It's a good idea to make sure you have a few one-euro coins when you arrive at the airport; you may need to pay for a baggage cart.

2 Words to remember (4 minutes)

il check-in *eel chekeen*	check-in
le partenze *lay partentsay*	departures
gli arrivi *lly arreevee*	arrivals
la dogana *lah doganah*	customs
il controllo passaporti *eel kontrolloh passaportee*	passport control
il terminale *eel termeenal*	terminal
l'uscita *loosheetah*	gate
il numero del volo *eel noomeroh del voloh*	flight number

Familiarize yourself with these words and test yourself using the cover flap.

Qual è l'uscita del volo per Roma?
kwalay loosheetah del voloh per rohmah
Which gate does the flight to Rome leave from?

3 Useful phrases (3 minutes)

Learn these phrases and then test yourself using the cover flap.

Il volo da Alghero è in orario? *eel voloh dah algayroh ay een orareeoh*	Is the flight from Alghero on time?
Non trovo i miei bagagli. *non trovoh ee mee-ayee bagallyee*	I can't find my baggage.
Il volo per Londra è in ritardo. *eel voloh per londrah ay een reetardoh*	The flight to London is delayed.

4 Put into practice (3 minutes)

Join in this conversation. Read the Italian on the left and follow the instructions to make your reply. Then test yourself by concealing the answers with the cover flap.

Buonasera. Dica?
bwonasayrah. dikah

Hello. Can I help you?

Ask: Is the flight to Milan on time?

Il volo per Milano è in orario?
eel voloh per meelanoh ay een orareeoh

Sì, signore.
see, seennyoray

Yes, sir.

Ask: Which gate does it leave from?

Qual è l'uscita del volo?
kwalay loosheetah del voloh

5 Match and repeat (4 minutes)

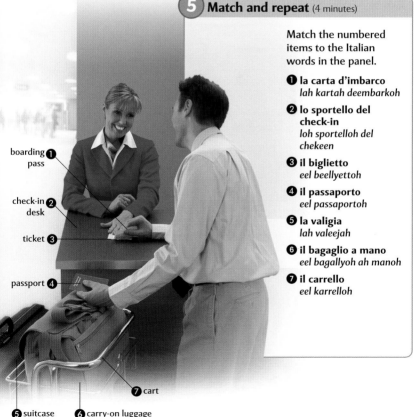

Match the numbered items to the Italian words in the panel.

1 la carta d'imbarco
lah kartah deembarkoh

2 lo sportello del check-in
loh sportelloh del chekeen

3 il biglietto
eel beellyettoh

4 il passaporto
eel passaportoh

5 la valigia
lah valeejah

6 il bagaglio a mano
eel bagallyoh ah manoh

7 il carrello
eel karrelloh

boarding pass 1

check-in desk 2

ticket 3

passport 4

7 cart

5 suitcase 6 carry-on luggage

RIPASSA E RIPETI
Review and repeat

1 **Places**

❶ **il museo**
eel moozayoh

❷ **il municipio**
eel mooneecheepeeoh

❸ **il ponte**
eel pontay

❹ **la piazza**
lah peeatsah

❺ **il parcheggio**
eel parkejjoh

❻ **il duomo**
eel dwomoh

❼ **il centro città**
eel chentroh cheettah

1 **Places** (4 minutes)

Name the numbered places in Italian.

❶ museum   ❷ town hall   ❸ bridge

❹ square   ❺ parking lot   ❻ cathedral

❼ downtown

2 **Car parts**

❶ **il parabrezza**
eel parabretsah

❷ **la freccia**
lah frechah

❸ **la gomma**
lah gommah

❹ **lo sportello**
loh sportelloh

❺ **il paraurti**
eel parahoortee

2 **Car parts** (3 minutes)

Name these car parts in Italian.

windshield ❶

❸ tire   ❹ door

3 Questions (4 minutes)

Ask the questions in Italian that match the following answers:

❶ Il pullman parte alle otto.

❷ Sono tre euro e venti.

❸ No grazie, non voglio vino.

❹ Il treno parte dal binario sette.

❺ Vado a Roma.

❻ Sì, il diciotto passa di qui.

❼ Il museo è in centro.

3 Questions

❶ A che ora parte il pullman?
ah kay orah partay eel poolman

❷ Quant'è?
kwantay

❸ Vuole del vino?
vwolay del veenoh

❹ Da quale binario parte il treno?
dah kwalay beenareeoh partay eel trenoh

❺ Dove va?
dovay vah

❻ Passa di qui il diciotto?
passah dee kwee eel deechottoh

❼ Dov'è il museo?
dovay eel moozayoh

4 Verbs (4 minutes)

❷ turn signal

❺ bumper

Fill in the blanks with the right form of the verb in brackets.

❶ (io) _____ scozzese. (essere)

❷ (noi) _____ l'autobus. (prendere)

❸ Il treno _____ a Verona. (andare)

❹ (loro) _____ tre bambine. (avere)

❺ (tu) _____ un tè? (volere)

❻ Quanti figli _____ signora? (avere)

4 Verbs

❶ sono
sonoh

❷ prendiamo
prendeeamoh

❸ va
vah

❹ hanno
annoh

❺ vuoi
vwoee

❻ ha
ah

1 Warm up (1 minute)

Ask "How much is that?" (pp.18-19) and "Do you accept credit cards?" (pp.38-9)

Ask "Do you have children?" (pp.12-13)

PRENOTARE UNA CAMERA
Booking a room

In Italy you can stay in a *standard hotel* (**l'albergo**). There is also the small, *family-run hotel* (**la pensione**), which is usually cheaper. Another option is a self-service *vacation apartment* (**l'appartamento per le vacanze**).

2 Useful phrases (3 minutes)

Practice these phrases and then test yourself by concealing the Italian on the left with the cover flap.

La colazione è compresa? *lah kolatseeonay ay komprezah*	Is breakfast included?
Accettate animali domestici? *acchayttatay aneemalee domesteechee*	Do you accept pets?
C'è il servizio in camera? *chay eel sayrveetsyoh een kamayrah*	Is there room service?
A che ora devo lasciare la camera? *ah kay orah devoh lasharay lah kamayrah*	What time do I have to check out?

3 In conversation (5 minutes)

Avete una camera?
avetay oonah kamayrah

Do you have any rooms?

Sì, abbiamo una matrimoniale.
see, abbeeamoh oonah matreemoneealay

Yes, we have a double room.

È possibile avere anche un lettino?
ay posseebeelay averay ankay oon letteenoh

Is it possible to get a crib, too?

4 Words to remember (4 minutes)

Familiarize yourself with these words and test yourself by concealing the Italian on the right with the cover flap.

La camera ha la vista sul parco?
lah kamayrah ah lah veestah sool parkoh
Does the room have a view over the park?

room	**la camera**	*lah kamayrah*
single room	**la camera singola**	*lah kamayrah seengolah*
double room	**la camera matrimoniale**	*lah kamayrah matreemoneealay*
twin room	**la camera a due letti**	*lah kamayrah ah dooay layttee*
bathroom	**il bagno**	*eel bannyoh*
shower	**la doccia**	*lah docchah*
breakfast	**la colazione**	*lah kolatseeonay*
key	**la chiave**	*lah keeavay*
balcony	**il balcone**	*eel balkonay*

5 Say it (2 minutes)

Do you have a single room, please?

For six nights.

Does the room have a balcony?

Cultural tip Generally in a hotel you have to pay extra if you want breakfast, but in a **pensione** it is included in the price. It usually consists of a choice of coffee or tea, pastries and/or bread with jam and butter, cereal, and juice.

Non c'è problema. Per quante notti?
non chay problemah. per kwantay nottee

No problem. How many nights?

Per tre notti.
per tray nottee

For three nights.

Benissimo. Ecco a Lei la chiave.
beneesseemoh. ekkoh ah lay lah keeavay

Very good. Here's the key.

1 Warm up (1 minute)

How do you say "Is there...?" and "There isn't..."? (pp.48-9)

What does "Dica?" mean? (pp.48-9)

IN ALBERGO
In the hotel

Although the larger hotels almost always have private bathrooms, there are still some **pensioni** where you will have to share the facilities. This can also be the case in some *youth hostels* (**ostelli della gioventù**), where a whole family can stay the night at a very reasonable cost.

2 Match and repeat (6 minutes)

Match the numbered items in this hotel bedroom with the Italian text in the panel and test yourself using the cover flap.

❶ **il comodino**
eel komodeenoh

❷ **la lampada**
lah lampadah

❸ **il mini bar**
eel meenee bar

❹ **le tende**
lay tenday

❺ **il divano**
eel deevanoh

❻ **il guanciale**
eel gwanchalay

❼ **il cuscino**
eel kusheenoh

❽ **il letto**
eel lettoh

❾ **il copriletto**
eel kopreelettoh

❿ **la coperta**
lah kopertah

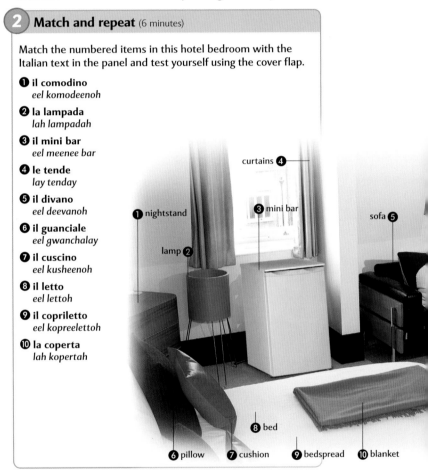

curtains ❹

❶ nightstand   ❸ mini bar   sofa ❺

lamp ❷

❽ bed

❻ pillow   ❼ cushion   ❾ bedspread   ❿ blanket

Cultural tip You'll find that the price of rooms varies according to the season, especially in tourist resorts. The highest prices are charged during *the high season* (**l'alta stagione**). Accommodation is generally much cheaper in *the low season* (**la bassa stagione**). It's a good idea to check before you book.

3 Useful phrases (5 minutes)

Learn these phrases and then test yourself using the cover flap.

The room is too cold/hot.	**In camera fa troppo freddo/caldo.** *een kamayrah fah troppoh freddoh/ kaldoh*
There are no towels.	**Non ci sono gli asciugamani.** *non chee sonoh lly ashugamanee*
I'd like some soap.	**Vorrei del sapone.** *vorray del saponay*
The shower doesn't work very well.	**La doccia non funziona bene.** *lah docchah non funtseeonah benay*
The elevator is not working.	**L'ascensore non funziona.** *lashensoray non funtseeonah*

4 Put into practice (3 minutes)

Cover the text on the right and then complete the dialogue in Italian.

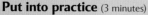

Buonasera. Dica? *bwonasayrah. deekah*	**Vorrei dei guanciali.** *vorray day gwanchalee*
Hello. Can I help you?	
Say: I'd like some pillows.	

La cameriera glieli porta subito. *lah kamereeayrah llyaylee portah soobeetoh*	**E la televisione non funziona.** *ay lah televeezeeonay non foontseeonah*
The maid will bring you some right away.	
Say: And the television doesn't work.	

Ask "Can I...?" (pp.34-5)

What is Italian for "the shower"? (pp.60-1)

Say "I'd like some towels." (pp.60-1)

IN CAMPEGGIO
At the campground

Camping is popular in Italy among Italians and visitors. Campgrounds are numerous and well organized. The local tourist office can usually provide a list of official campgrounds in the area where you plan to stay. Respect any signs announcing **campeggio vietato** (*camping forbidden*).

2 **Useful phrases** (3 minutes)

Learn these phrases and then test yourself by concealing the Italian with the cover flap.

È possibile noleggiare una bicicletta? *ay posseebeelay nolayjjaray oonah beecheeklettah*	Can I rent a bicycle?
L'acqua è potabile? *lahkkwah ay potabeelay*	Is this drinking water?
È permesso accendere i falò? *ay permessoh acchenderay ee faloh*	Are campfires allowed?
È proibito giocare a pallone. *ay proeebeetoh jokaray ah pallonay*	Ball games are forbidden.

Il campeggio è tranquillo.
eel kampayjjoh ay trankweelloh
The campground is quiet.

la direzione del campeggio
lah deeraytseeonay del kampayjjoh
campground office

i rifiuti
ee reefeeootee
trash can

il telo protettivo
eel teloh protetteevoh
flysheet

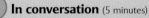

3 **In conversation** (5 minutes)

Vorremmo una piazzola per tre notti.
vorremmoh oonah peeatsolah per tray nottee

I need a site for three nights.

Ce n'è una vicino alla piscina.
chay nay oonah veecheenoh allah peesheenah

There's one near the swimming pool.

Quant'è?
kwantay

How much is it?

5 Say it (2 minutes)

I need a site for four nights.

Can I rent a tent?

Where's the electrical hookup?

4 Words to remember (4 minutes)

Familiarize yourself with these words and test yourself using the cover flap.

tent	**la tenda**	*lah tendah*
camper trailer	**la roulotte**	*lah roolott*
camper van	**il camper**	*eel kamper*
air mattress	**il materassino gonfiabile**	*eel matayraseenoh gonfeeyabeelay*
sleeping bag	**il sacco a pelo**	*eel sakkoh ah peloh*
site	**la piazzola**	*lah peeatsolah*
campfire	**il falò**	*eel faloh*
drinking water	**l'acqua potabile (f)**	*lahkkwah potabeelay*
garbage	**l'immondizia (f)**	*leemmondeetseeah*
showers	**le docce**	*lay docchay*
flashlight	**la torcia**	*lah torchah*
backpack	**lo zaino**	*loh tsa-eenoh*
stove fuel	**il gas da campeggio**	*eel gas dah kampayjjoh*

i bagni
ee banyee
restrooms

la presa di corrente
lah praysah dee korrentay
electrical hookup

la corda
lah kordah
guy rope

il picchetto
eel peekettoh
peg

Cinquanta euro, una notte anticipata.
cheenkwantah ehooroh, oonah nottay anteecheepatah

Fifty euros, one night in advance.

È possibile affittare un barbecue?
ay posseebeelay affeettaray oon barbeku

Can I rent a barbecue grill?

Sì, ma deve versare una cauzione.
see, mah devay versaray oonah kaootseeonay

Yes, but you must pay a deposit.

DESCRIZIONE
Descriptions

How do you say "hot" and "cold"? (pp.60-1)

What is the Italian for "bedroom," "bed," and "pillow"? (pp.60-1)

Adjectives are words used to describe people, things, and places. In Italian you generally put the adjective after the thing it describes—for example, **una camera singola** (*a single room*), but you will sometimes see them placed before—for example, **una bella donna** (*a beautiful woman*).

2 **Words to remember** (7 minutes)

Adjectives usually change depending on whether the thing described is masculine, feminine, masculine plural, or feminine plural. In most cases, adjectives end in **-o** for masculine singular words and **-a** for the feminine. Plural endings are **-i** for masculine and **-e** for feminine. Some adjectives end in **-e** for the masculine and the feminine, changing to **-i** in the plural. Others never change.

Le montagne sono alte.
lay montanyay sonoh altay
The mountains are high.

grande *granday*	big, large
piccolo/piccola *peekkoloh/peekkolah*	small
alto/alta *altoh/altah*	high, tall
basso/bassa *bassoh/bassah*	short
caldo/calda *kaldoh/kaldah*	hot
freddo/fredda *freddoh/freddah*	cold
buono/buona *bwonoh/bwonah*	good
cattivo/cattiva *katteevoh/katteevah*	bad
lento/lenta *lentoh/lentah*	slow
veloce *velochay*	fast
duro/dura *dooroh/doorah*	hard
morbido/morbida *morbeedoh/morbeedah*	soft
bello/bella *belloh/bellah*	beautiful
brutto/brutta *broottoh/broottah*	ugly

La chiesa è vecchia.
lah keeayzah eh vekkeeah
The church is old.

La casa è piccola.
lah kasah ay peekkolah
The house is small.

Il paese è molto bello.
eel pahesay ay moltoh belloh
The village is very beautiful.

3 Useful phrases (4 minutes)

You can emphasize a description by using **molto** (*very*), **troppo** (*too*), or **più** (*more*) before the adjective.

The coffee is cold.	**Il caffè è freddo.** *eel kaffay ay freddoh*
My room is very noisy.	**La mia camera è molto rumorosa.** *lah mee-ah kamayrah ay moltoh roomorosah*
The car is too small.	**L'auto è troppo piccola.** *la-ootoh ay troppoh peekkolah*
I'd like a softer bed.	**Vorrei un letto più morbido.** *vorray oon lettoh peeoo morbeedoh*

4 Put into practice (3 minutes)

Join in this conversation. Cover up the text on the right and complete the dialogue in Italian. Check and repeat if necessary.

Ecco la camera. *ekkoh lah kamayrah* Here is the bedroom. Say: The view is very beautiful.	**La vista è molto bella.** *lah veestah ay moltoh bellah*
Il bagno è là. *eel bannyoh ay lah* The bathroom is over there. Say: It is too small.	**È troppo piccolo.** *ay troppoh peekkoloh*
Non abbiamo altre camere. *non abbeeamoh altray kamayray* We don't have any other rooms. Say: We'll take it.	**La prendiamo.** *lah prendeeamoh*

RIPASSA E RIPETI
Review and repeat

1 Adjectives

❶ **piccola**
peekkolah

❷ **morbido**
morbeedoh

❸ **buono**
bwonoh

❹ **freddo**
freddoh

❺ **grande**
granday

1 Adjectives (3 minutes)

Put the word in brackets into Italian using the correct masculine or feminine form.

❶ La camera è troppo _____. (small)

❷ Vorrei un guanciale più _____. (soft)

❸ Il caffè è molto _____. (good)

❹ In questo bagno fa _____. (cold)

❺ Vorrei un letto più _____. (big)

2 Campsite

❶ **la presa di corrente**
lah praysah dee korrentay

❷ **la tenda**
lah tendah

❸ **i rifiuti**
ee reefeeootee

❹ **la corda**
lah kordah

❺ **i bagni**
ee banyee

❻ **la roulotte**
lah roolott

2 Campsite (3 minutes)

Name these items you might find in a campground.

tent ❷

guy rope ❹

electrical ❶
hookup

trash can ❸

3 At the hotel (4 minutes)

You are booking a room in a hotel. Follow the conversation, replying in Italian following the English prompts.

Buongiorno.
❶ Do you have a double room?

Sì. Per quante notti?
❷ Three nights. Do you accept pets?

Certo.
❸ Is breakfast included?

No. Sono cinque euro.
❹ That's fine. We'll take it.

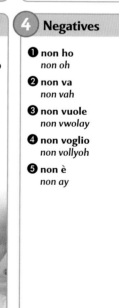

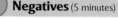

3 At the hotel

❶ **Avete una camera matrimoniale?**
avetay oonah kamerah matreemonyalay

❷ **Tre notti. Accettate animali domestici?**
tray nottee. acchayttatay aneemalee domesteechee

❸ **La colazione è compresa?**
lah kolatseeonay ay komprezah

❹ **Va bene. La prendiamo.**
vah benay. lah prendeeamoh

4 Negatives (5 minutes)

Make these sentences negative using the correct form of the verb in brackets.

❶ (io) _____ figli. (avere)

❷ (Lei) _____ a Genova domani. (andare)

❸ (lui) _____ vino. (volere)

❹ (io) _____ lo zucchero nel caffè. (volere)

❺ La camera _____ molto bella. (essere)

4 Negatives

❶ **non ho**
non oh

❷ **non va**
non vah

❸ **non vuole**
non vwolay

❹ **non voglio**
non vollyoh

❺ **non è**
non ay

❺ restrooms

❻ camper trailer

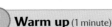

1 Warm up (1 minute)

Ask "How do I get to the station?" (pp.50-1)

Say "Turn left at the traffic lights," and "The station is across from the café." (pp.50-1)

I NEGOZI
Shops

Small, traditional specialized stores are still very common in Italy. But you can also find big supermarkets and shopping malls on the outskirts of cities. Local markets selling fresh, local produce can be found everywhere. You can find out the market day at the tourist office.

2 Match and repeat (5 minutes)

Match the stores numbered 1-9 below and right to the Italian in the panel. Then test yourself using the cover flap.

❶ la panetteria
lah panettayreeah

❷ la pasticceria
lah pastee-chayreeah

❸ gli alimentari
lly aleementaree

❹ la salumeria
lah saloomay-reeah

❺ il tabaccaio
eel tabakkaeeoh

❻ la libreria
lah leebrayreeah

❼ la pescheria
lah payskayreeah

❽ la macelleria
lah machayllay-reeah

❾ la banca
lah bankah

❶ bread shop

❷ bakery

❹ delicatessen

❺ tobacconist

❼ fishmonger

❽ butcher shop

Cultural tip Although most Italian pharmacies also sell cosmetics and toiletries, the best shop in which to buy these items is **la profumeria**. Some are very upmarket and offer a wider range of brands. **Il tabaccaio** (tobacconist) is the only licensed outlet for cigarettes and stamps (except the post office in the case of stamps). Sometimes you will find a tobacconist counter within the premises of a bar.

Dov'è il fioraio?
dovay eel feeoraeeoh
Where is the florist?

3 Words to remember (4 minutes)

Familiarize yourself with these words and then test yourself.

dairy	**la latteria** *lah lattereeah*
wine shop	**l'enoteca (f)** *laynotekah*
antique shop	**l'antiquario (m)** *lanteekwareeoh*
hairdresser	**il parrucchiere** *eel parrookyayray*
jeweler	**la gioielleria** *la joyayllereeah*
post office	**le poste** *lay postay*
leather goods shop	**la pelletteria** *lah pellettereeah*
travel agent	**l'agenzia di viaggi** *lajentseeah dee veeajjee*
shoe repairer	**il calzolaio** *eel kaltsolaeeoh*

❸ grocery store

❻ bookstore

❾ bank

4 Useful phrases (3 minutes)

Familiarize yourself with these phrases.

Where is the hairdresser?	**Dov'è il parrucchiere?** *dovay eel parrookyayray*
Where do I pay?	**Dove pago?** *dovay pagoh*
I'm just looking, thank you.	**Do solo un'occhiata, grazie.** *doh soloh oonokyatah, gratseeay*
Do you sell SIM cards?	**Avete carte SIM?** *avetay kartay seem*
Can I exchange this?	**Posso cambiare questo?** *possoh kambeearay kwestoh*
Can you give me the receipt?	**Mi dà lo scontrino?** *mee dah loh skontreenoh*
I'd like to place an order.	**Vorrei fare un'ordinazione.** *vorray faray oonordeenatseeonay*

5 Say it (2 minutes)

Where is the bank?

Do you sell cheese?

Where do I pay?

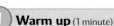

AL MERCATO
At the market

Italy uses the metric system of weights and measures. You need to ask for produce in *kilograms*—**chili** for short—or grams. Some larger items tend to be priced individually, **l'uno** (each). In many Italian markets you will find foodstuffs and also stands selling clothing and household goods.

2 **Match and repeat** (4 minutes)

Match the numbered items in this scene with the text in the panel.

❶ **il finocchio**
eel feenokeeoh

❷ **il cavolfiore**
eel kavolfeeoray

❸ **la lattuga**
lah lattoogah

❹ **i peperoni**
ee paypaironee

❺ **le patate**
lay patatay

❻ **l'aglio (m)**
lalyoh

❼ **i pomodori**
ee pomodoree

❽ **gli asparagi**
lly asparajee

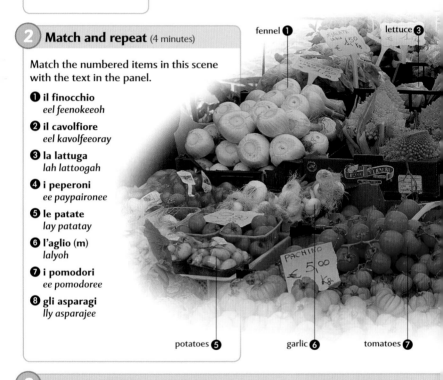

fennel ❶
lettuce ❸
potatoes ❺
garlic ❻
tomatoes ❼

3 **In conversation** (3 minutes)

Vorrei dei pomodori.
vorray day pomodoree

I'd like some tomatoes.

Quanti chili?
kwantee keelee

How many kilos?

Due chili, per favore.
dooay keelee, per favoray

Two kilos, please.

Cultural tip Italy uses the European currency, the euro. This is divided into 100 cents, which the Italians call **centesimi**. You will usually hear the price given as **dieci euro e venti** (€10,20), **sei euro e novantanove** (€6,99), etc. Italians use a comma for the decimal point.

4 Useful phrases (5 minutes)

Learn these phrases. Then conceal the answers on the right using the cover flap. Read the English under the pictures and say the phrase in Italian as shown on the right.

asparagus **8** **2** cauliflower

peppers **4**

Quel formaggio è troppo caro.
kwel formajjoh ay troppoh karoh

That cheese is too expensive.

Quanto costa quello lì?
kwantoh kostah kwelloh lee

How much is that one?

5 Say it (2 minutes)

Three kilos of potatoes, please.

The peppers are too expensive.

How much is the lettuce?

Basta così.
bastah kosee

That's all.

Altro, signore?
altroh, seennyoray

Anything else, sir?

Basta così, grazie. Quant'è?
bastah kozee, gratseeay. kwantay

That's all, thank you. How much?

Due euro e cinquanta.
dooay ayooroh ay cheenkwantah

Two euros fifty.

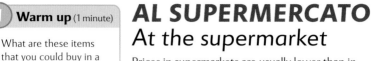

AL SUPERMERCATO
At the supermarket

1 **Warm up** (1 minute)

What are these items that you could buy in a supermarket? (pp.24-5)

la carne

il pesce

il formaggio

il succo di frutta

il vino

l'acqua

Prices in supermarkets are usually lower than in smaller shops. They offer all kinds of products, with larger out-of-town **ipermercati** (*large supermarkets*) carrying clothes, household goods, garden furniture, and home improvement products. They may also stock regional products.

2 **Match and repeat** (5 minutes)

Look at the numbered items and match them to the Italian words in the panel on the left.

❶ gli articoli per la casa
lly arteekolee per lah kazah

❷ la frutta
lah froottah

❸ le bibite
lay beebeetay

❹ i piatti pronti
ee pyattee prontee

❺ i cosmetici
ee kosmeteechee

❻ i latticini
ee latteecheenee

❼ la verdura
lah verdoorah

❽ i surgelati
ee soorjelatee

household products **❶**

fruit **❷**

drinks **❸**

prepared meals **❹**

vegetables **❼**

frozen foods **❽**

Cultural tip It is not usually possible to take unweighed fruit and vegetables sold by the kilo directly to the supermarket checkout. There is usually a self-service weighing machine.

3 **Useful phrases** (3 minutes)

Learn these phrases and then test yourself using the cover flap.

May I have a bag, please?	**Posso avere un sacchetto, per favore?** *possoh avayray oon sakkayttoh, per favoray*
Where is the liquor aisle?	**Qual è la fila delle bibite?** *kwalay lah feelah dellay beebeetay*
Where is the checkout, please?	**Dov'è la cassa?** *dovay lah kassah*
Please type in your PIN.	**Può battere il pin.** *pwoh battayray eel pin*

5 beauty products

6 dairy products

5 **Say it** (2 minutes)

Where's the dairy products aisle?

May I have some ham, please?

Where are the frozen foods?

4 **Words to remember** (4 minutes)

Learn these words and then test yourself using the cover flap.

bread	**il pane** *eel panay*
milk	**il latte** *eel lattay*
butter	**il burro** *eel boorroh*
ham	**il prosciutto** *eel proshoottoh*
salt	**il sale** *eel salay*
pepper	**il pepe** *eel paypay*
toilet paper	**la carta igienica** *lah kartah eejeneekah*
diapers	**i pannolini** *ee pannoleenee*
dishwashing liquid	**il detersivo per i piatti** *eel deterseevoh per ee pyattee*

Warm up (1 minute)

Say "I'd like… ." (pp.22-3)

Ask "Do you have…?"
(pp.14-15)

Say "38," "42," and "46."
(pp.30-1)

Say "big" and "small."
(pp.64-5)

SCARPE E ABBIGLIAMENTO
Clothes and shoes

Clothes and shoes are measured in metric sizes. Even allowing for conversion of sizes, Italian clothes tend to be cut very small. Note that clothes size is **la taglia** but shoe size is **il numero**.

2 Match and repeat (3 minutes)

Match the numbered items of clothing to the Italian words in the panel on the left. Test yourself using the cover flap.

❶ **la camicia**
   lah kameechah

❷ **la cravatta**
   lah kravattah

❸ **la giacca**
   lah jakkah

❹ **la tasca**
   lah taskah

❺ **la manica**
   lah maneekah

❻ **i pantaloni**
   ee pantalonee

❼ **la gonna**
   lah gonnah

❽ **i collant**
   ee kollant

❾ **le scarpe**
   lay skarpay

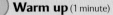

shirt ❶

tie ❷

jacket ❸

pocket ❹

sleeve ❺

pants ❻

Cultural tip Like most of Europe, Italy uses the continental system of sizes. Italian dress sizes usually range from 36 (US 6) through to 48 (US 14) and shoe sizes from 37 (US 5 ½) to 46 (US 12). For men's shirts, a size 41 is a 16-inch collar, 43 is a 17-inch collar, and 45 is an 18-inch collar.

3 Put into practice (4 minutes)

Join in this conversation. Use the cover flap to conceal the text on the right and complete the dialogue in Italian.

Che lavoro fa?
kay lavoroh fah

What do you do?

Say: I am a financial consultant.

Sono consulente finanziario.
sonoh konsoolentay feenantseearyoh

Per quale azienda lavora?
per kwalay adzyendah lavorah

What company do you work for?

Say: I'm self-employed.

Sono libero professionista.
sonoh leeberoh professyoneestah

Interessante!
eenteressantay

How interesting!

Ask: What is your profession?

E Lei che lavoro fa?
ay lay kay lavoroh fah

Sono dentista.
sonoh denteestah

I'm a dentist.

Say: My sister is a dentist, too.

Anche mia sorella è dentista.
ankay mee-ah sorellah ay denteestah

4 Words to remember: workplace (3 minutes)

La sede centrale è a Napoli.
lah seday chentralay ay ah napolee
Headquarters is in Naples.

Familiarize yourself with these words and test yourself.

headquarters	**la sede centrale** *lah seday chentralay*
branch	**la filiale** *lah feelyalay*
department	**il reparto** *eel repartoh*
office worker	**l'impiegato/a** *leempyegatoh/ah*
manager	**il direttore/la direttrice** *eel deerettoray/lah deerettreechay*

L'UFFICIO
The office

An office environment or business situation has
its own vocabulary in any language, but there are
many items for which the terminology is virtually
universal. Be aware that Italian computer keyboards
may have a different layout from the standard US
QWERTY convention.

2 **Words to remember** (5 minutes)

Familiarize yourself with these words. Read them aloud several
times and try to memorize them. Conceal the Italian with the
cover flap and test yourself.

il computer *eel komputer*	computer
il mouse *eel maoos*	mouse
l'email (f) *leemayl*	email
internet (f) *eenternet*	internet
la password *lah password*	password
la segreteria telefonica *lah segretereeah telayfoneekah*	voicemail
la password del wifi *lah password dell weefee*	Wi-Fi code
la fotocopiatrice *lah fotokopyatreechay*	photocopier
l'agenda (f) *lajendah*	planner
il biglietto da visita *eel beellyettoh dah veeseetah*	business card
la riunione *lah reeoonyonay*	meeting
la conferenza *lah konferentsah*	conference
l'ordine del giorno (m) *lordeenay del jornoh*	agenda

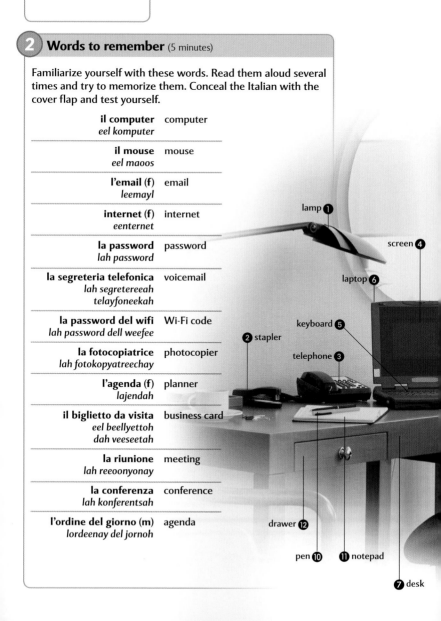

lamp **1**

screen **4**

laptop **6**

keyboard **5**

2 stapler

telephone **3**

drawer **12**

pen **10**　　**11** notepad

7 desk

3 Useful phrases (2 minutes)

Learn these phrases and then test yourself using the cover flap.

I need to make some photocopies.	**Ho bisogno di fare delle fotocopie.** *oh beezonnyoh dee faray dellay fotokopyay*
I'd like to make an appointment.	**Vorrei fissare un appuntamento.** *vorray feessaray oon appoontamentoh*
I want to send an email.	**Voglio mandare un'email.** *vollyoh mandaray oon eemayl*

4 Match and repeat (5 minutes)

Match the numbered items to the Italian words on the right.

5 Say it (2 minutes)

I'd like to arrange a meeting.

Do you have a business card?

I have a laptop.

clock **8**

printer **9**

13 swivel chair

1 la lampada
lah lampadah

2 la spillatrice
lah speellatreechay

3 il telefono
eel telayfonoh

4 lo schermo
loh skayrmoh

5 la tastiera
lah tastyerah

6 il computer portatile
eel komputer portateelay

7 la scrivania
lah skreevaneeah

8 l'orologio (m)
lorolojoh

9 la stampante
lah stampantay

10 la penna
lah pennah

11 il bloc-notes
eel bloknotays

12 il cassetto
eel kassettoh

13 la sedia girevole
lah sedya jeerayvolay

IL MONDO ACCADEMICO
Academic world

1 **Warm up** (1 minute)

Say "How interesting!" (pp.78-9), "library" (pp.48-9), and "appointment." (pp.32-3)

Ask "What is your profession?" and answer "I'm an accountant." (pp.78-9)

Italian students may take a short degree course, **la laurea breve**. There is also a longer course, **la laurea**, equivalent to a master's degree. The title **dottore** or **dottoressa** is used by all graduates and most professionals.

2 **Useful phrases** (3 minutes)

Learn these phrases and then test yourself using the cover flap.

Di cosa si occupa? *dee kozah see okkoopah*	What is your field?
Mi occupo di ricerca scientifica. *mee okkoopoh dee reecherkah shenteefeekah*	I am doing scientific research.
Sono laureato in legge. *sonoh laooreatoh een lejjay*	I have a degree in law.
Tengo una conferenza sull'architettura moderna. *tayngoh oonah konferentsah soollarkeetettoorah modernah*	I am giving a lecture on modern architecture.

3 **In conversation** (5 minutes)

Buongiorno, sono la professoressa Lanzi.
bwonjornoh, sonoh lah professoressah lantsee

Hello, I'm Professor Lanzi.

Dove insegna?
dovay eensennyah

Where do you teach?

Insegno all'università di Pisa.
eensennyoh allooneeverseetah dee pisah

I teach at the University of Pisa.

4 Words to remember (4 minutes)

Familiarize yourself with these words and then test yourself.

Abbiamo uno stand alla fiera commerciale.
abbyamoh oonoh stend allah fyerah kommerchalay
We have a stand at the trade fair.

conference/lecture	**la conferenza** *lah konferentsah*
seminar	**il seminario** *eel semeenaryoh*
conference room	**la sala conferenze** *lah salah konferentsay*
lecture hall	**l'aula delle lezioni (f)** *laoolah dellay letseeonee*
exhibition	**la mostra** *lah mostrah*
associate professor	**il professore universitario/ la professoressa universitaria** *eel professoray ooneeverseetareeoh/ lah professoressah ooneeverseetaryah*
medicine	**la medicina** *lah medeecheenah*
science	**la scienza** *lah schentsah*
literature	**la letteratura** *lah letteratoorah*
engineering	**l'ingegneria (f)** *leenjennyereeah*
information technology	**l'informatica (f)** *leenformateekah*

5 Say it (2 minutes)

I'm doing research in medicine.

I have a degree in literature.

She's the professor.

Di cosa si occupa?
dee kozah see okkoopah

What's your field?

Di fisica. Mi occupo di ricerca.
dee feeseekah. mee okkoopoh dee reecherkah

Physics. I'm doing research.

Interessante!
eenteressantay

How interesting!

1 Warm up (1 minute)

Ask "Can I...?" (pp.34-5)

Say "I want to send an email." (pp.80-1)

Say "I'd like to make an appointment." (pp.80-1)

I CONTATTI COMMERCIALI
In business

You will make a good impression if you make the effort to begin a meeting with a few words in Italian, even if your vocabulary is limited. After that, all parties will probably be happy to continue in English.

2 Words to remember (6 minutes)

Familiarize yourself with these words and then test yourself by concealing the Italian with the cover flap.

l'ordinativo (m) *lordeenateevoh*	order
la consegna *lah konsennyah*	delivery
il pagamento *eel pagamentoh*	payment
il budget *eel bajjet*	budget
il prezzo *eel pretsoh*	price
i documenti *ee dokoomentee*	documents
la fattura *lah fattoorah*	invoice
il preventivo *eel preventeevoh*	estimate
i profitti *ee profeettee*	profits
le vendite *lay vendeetay*	sales
le cifre *lay cheefray*	figures

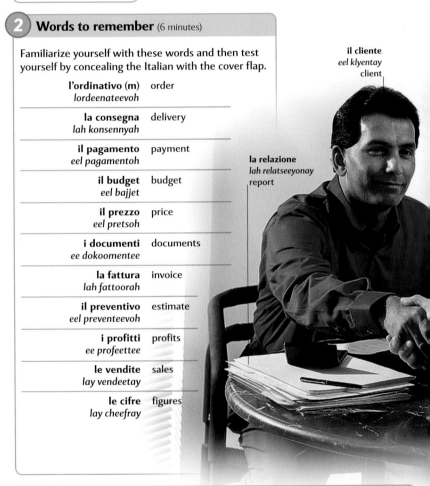

il cliente
eel klyentay
client

la relazione
lah relatseeyonay
report

Cultural tip In general, business dealings are formal, but a long lunch with wine is still a feature of doing business in Italy. As a client, you can expect to be taken out to a restaurant, and as a supplier you should consider entertaining your customers.

3 **Useful phrases** (6 minutes)

Practice these phrases. Notice the use of the word **può** (*can you*) as a preface to polite requests.

Firmiamo il contratto?
feermyamoh eel kontrattoh
Shall we sign the contract?

il dirigente
eel deereejentay
executive

il contratto
eel kontrattoh
contract

Può mandarmi il contratto, per favore?
pwoh mandarmee eel kontrattoh, per favoray

Can you send me the contract, please?

Abbiamo fissato il prezzo?
abbeeamoh feessatoh eel pretsoh

Have we agreed on a price?

Quando può effettuare la consegna?
kwandoh pwoh effettwaray lah konsennyah

When can you make the delivery?

Quant'è il budget?
kwantay eel bajjet

What's the budget?

Può mandarmi la fattura?
pwoh mandarmee lah fattoorah

Can you send me the invoice?

4 **Say it** (2 minutes)

Can you send me the estimate?

Have we agreed on a budget?

When can you send me the contract?

RIPASSA E RIPETI
Review and repeat

Risposte
Answers (Cover with flap)

1 At the office

❶ **la spillatrice**
lah speellatreechay

❷ **la lampada**
lah lampadah

❸ **il computer portatile**
eel komputer portateelay

❹ **la penna**
lah pennah

❺ **la scrivania**
lah skreevaneeah

❻ **il bloc-notes**
eel bloknotays

❼ **l'orologio (m)**
lorolojoh

1 At the office (4 minutes)

Name these items in Italian.

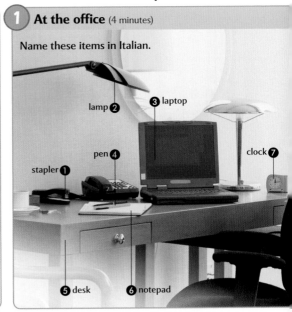

lamp ❷ ❸ laptop

pen ❹ clock ❼

stapler ❶

❺ desk ❻ notepad

2 Jobs

❶ **medico**
medeekoh

❷ **idraulico**
eedraooleekoh

❸ **commerciante**
kommerchantay

❹ **ragioniere/a**
rajonyeray/ah

❺ **studente/essa**
stoodentay/essah

❻ **avvocato**
avvokatoh

2 Jobs (3 minutes)

What are these jobs in Italian?

❶ doctor

❷ plumber

❸ shopkeeper

❹ accountant

❺ student

❻ lawyer

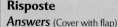

3 Work (4 minutes)

Answer these questions following the English prompts.

Per quale azienda lavora?
❶ Say "I work for myself."

Dove insegna?
❷ Say "I teach at the University of Pisa."

Di cosa si occupa?
❸ Say "I'm doing scientific research."

Quando può mandare il preventivo?
❹ Say "I can send the estimate tomorrow."

3 Work

❶ **Sono libero professionista.**
sonoh leeberoh professyoneestah

❷ **Insegno all'università di Pisa.**
eensennyoh allooneeverseetah dee pisah

❸ **Mi occupo di ricerca scientifica.**
mee okkoopoh dee reecherkah sheenteefeekah

❹ **Posso mandare il preventivo domani.**
possoh mandaray eel preventeevoh domanee

4 How much? (4 minutes)

Answer the question with the price shown in brackets.

❶ **Quant'è un caffè?** (€1,80)

❷ **Quanto costa la camera?** (€47)

❸ **Quanto costa un chilo di pomodori?** (€1,25)

❹ **Quanto costa una piazzola per tre giorni?** (€50)

4 How much?

❶ **Un euro e ottanta**
oon ayooroh ay ottantah

❷ **Quarantasette euro**
kwarantasettay ayooroh

❸ **Un euro e venticinque**
oon ayooroh ay venteecheenkway

❹ **Cinquanta euro**
cheenkwantah ayooroh

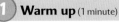

Warm up (1 minute)

Say "I'm allergic to nuts." (pp.24-5)

Say the verb "avere" (to have) in all its forms (io, tu, Lei, lui/lei, noi, voi, loro) (pp.14-15).

IN FARMACIA
At the pharmacy

Italian pharmacists study for over four years to get their licenses, and they can give advice about minor health problems and are permitted to dispense a wide variety of medicines, even giving injections, if necessary. There is a *duty pharmacist* (**farmacia di turno**) in most towns.

2 Match and repeat (3 minutes)

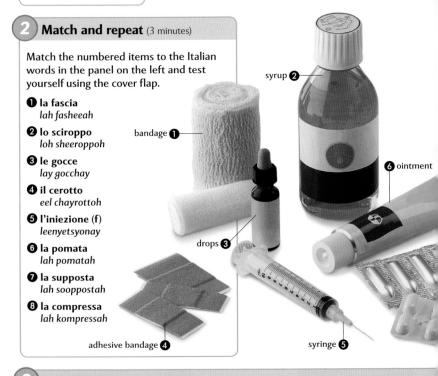

Match the numbered items to the Italian words in the panel on the left and test yourself using the cover flap.

1 **la fascia**
lah fasheeah

2 **lo sciroppo**
loh sheeroppoh

3 **le gocce**
lay gocchay

4 **il cerotto**
eel chayrottoh

5 **l'iniezione** (f)
leenyetsyonay

6 **la pomata**
lah pomatah

7 **la supposta**
lah sooppostah

8 **la compressa**
lah kompressah

syrup **2**

bandage **1**

6 ointment

drops **3**

adhesive bandage **4**

syringe **5**

3 In conversation (3 minutes)

Buongiorno. Dica?
bwonjornoh. deekah

Hello. What would you like?

Ho mal di pancia.
oh mal dee panchah

I have a stomachache.

Ha anche la diarrea?
ah ankay lah deearreah

Do you also have diarrhea?

4 Words to remember (2 minutes)

Familiarize yourself with these words and test yourself using the cover flap.

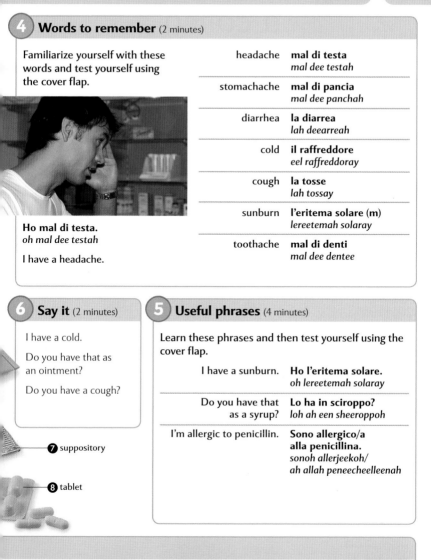

Ho mal di testa.
oh mal dee testah

I have a headache.

headache	**mal di testa** *mal dee testah*
stomachache	**mal di pancia** *mal dee panchah*
diarrhea	**la diarrea** *lah deearreah*
cold	**il raffreddore** *eel raffreddoray*
cough	**la tosse** *lah tossay*
sunburn	**l'eritema solare (m)** *lereetemah solaray*
toothache	**mal di denti** *mal dee dentee*

6 Say it (2 minutes)

I have a cold.

Do you have that as an ointment?

Do you have a cough?

7 suppository

8 tablet

5 Useful phrases (4 minutes)

Learn these phrases and then test yourself using the cover flap.

I have a sunburn.	**Ho l'eritema solare.** *oh lereetemah solaray*
Do you have that as a syrup?	**Lo ha in sciroppo?** *loh ah een sheeroppoh*
I'm allergic to penicillin.	**Sono allergico/a alla penicillina.** *sonoh allerjeekoh/ ah allah peneecheelleenah*

No, ma ho mal di testa.
noh, mah oh mal dee testah

No, but I have a headache.

Prenda questo.
prendah kwestoh

Take this.

Lo ha in compresse?
loh ah een kompressay

Do you have that as tablets?

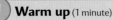

1 Warm up (1 minute)

Say " I have a toothache" and "I have a sunburn." (pp.88-9)

Say the Italian for "red," "green," "black," and "yellow." (pp.74-5)

IL CORPO
The body

A common phrase for talking about aches and pains is **mi fa male il/la**... (*my ... hurts*). Another useful expression is **ho un dolore a**... (*I have a pain in...*). Note that **a** joins with the definite article (*the*) to produce these combinations: **il** (**al**), **lo** (**allo**), **la** (**alla**), **gli** (**agli**), **i** (**ai**), and **le** (**alle**).

2 Match and repeat: body (6 minutes)

Match the numbered parts of the body with the list on the left. Test yourself by using the cover flap.

1 la mano
lah manoh

2 la testa
lah testah

3 la spalla
la spallah

4 il gomito
eel gomeetoh

5 i capelli
ee kapellee

6 il braccio
eel brachoh

7 il collo
eel kolloh

8 il petto
eel pettoh

9 lo stomaco
loh stomakoh

10 la gamba
lah gambah

11 il ginocchio
eel jeenokkyoh

12 il piede
eel pyeday

1 hand
4 elbow
5 hair
2 head
6 arm
shoulder 3
7 neck
chest 8
stomach 9
leg 10
knee 11
12 foot

3 Match and repeat: face (3 minutes)

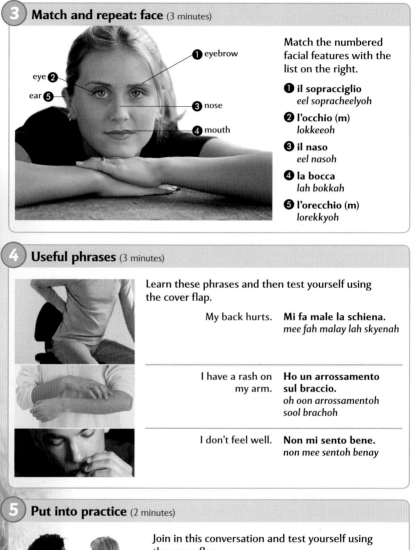

1 eyebrow

eye **2**

ear **5**

3 nose

4 mouth

Match the numbered facial features with the list on the right.

1 il sopracciglio
eel sopracheelyoh

2 l'occhio (m)
lokkeeoh

3 il naso
eel nasoh

4 la bocca
lah bokkah

5 l'orecchio (m)
lorekkyoh

4 Useful phrases (3 minutes)

Learn these phrases and then test yourself using the cover flap.

My back hurts.	**Mi fa male la schiena.** *mee fah malay lah skyenah*
I have a rash on my arm.	**Ho un arrossamento sul braccio.** *oh oon arrossamentoh sool brachoh*
I don't feel well.	**Non mi sento bene.** *non mee sentoh benay*

5 Put into practice (2 minutes)

Join in this conversation and test yourself using the cover flap.

Cosa c'è? **Non mi sento bene.**
kozah chay *non mee sentoh benay*

What's the matter?

Say: I don't feel well.

Dove ti fa male? **Ho un dolore alla spalla.**
dovay ti fah malay *oh oon doloray*
allah spallah

Where does it hurt?

Say: I have a pain in my shoulder.

DAL MEDICO
At the doctor

Unless it's an emergency, you'll have to make an appointment with the doctor and pay when you leave. You may be able to reclaim the cost if you have medical insurance. Find the names and addresses of local doctors from **il municipio** (*town hall*), or ask at a local pharmacy.

2 Useful phrases you may hear (3 minutes)

Learn these phrases and then test yourself using the cover flap to conceal the Italian on the left.

Non è grave. *non ay gravay*	It's not serious.
Deve fare dei controlli. *devay faray day kontrollee*	You need to have tests.
Ha una frattura. *ah oonah frattoorah*	You have a fracture.
Deve andare all'ospedale. *devay andaray allospedalay*	You need to go to the hospital.

Fa qualche cura?
fah kwalkay koorah
Are you taking any medication?

3 In conversation (5 minutes)

Cosa c'è?
kozah chay

What's the matter?

Ho un dolore al petto.
oh oon doloray al pettoh

I have a pain in my chest.

Ora la visito.
orah lah veezeetoh

Now I will examine you.

4 Useful phrases you may need to say (4 minutes)

Learn these phrases and then test yourself using the cover flap.

I am diabetic.	**Sono diabetico/a.** *sonoh deeabeteekoh/ah*
I am epileptic.	**Sono epilettico/a.** *sonoh epeeletteekoh/ah*
I have asthma.	**Sono asmatico/a.** *sonoh asmateekoh/ah*
I have a heart condition.	**Ho disturbi cardiaci.** *oh deestoorbee* *kardeeachee*
I have a fever.	**Ho la febbre.** *oh lah febbray*
It's urgent.	**È urgente.** *ay oorjentay*
I'm out of breath.	**Faccio fatica** **a respirare.** *facchyoh fatikah* *ah respeeraray*

Sono incinta.
sonoh eencheentah
I am pregnant.

Cultural tip

Before you go to Italy, find out if your health insurance covers emergency medical care in Europe; if it doesn't, purchase a travel medical insurance policy. For an ambulance call 112.

5 Say it (2 minutes)

My son needs to go to the hospital.

It's not urgent.

È grave?
ay gravay

Is it serious?

No, è solo un'indigestione.
noh, ay soloh
oon eendeejestyonay

No, you only have indigestion.

Che sollievo!
kay soleeayvoh

What a relief!

1 **Warm up** (1 minute)

Say "There's an elevator over there." (pp.52-3)

Ask "Do I need...?" (pp.92-3)

What is the Italian for "mouth" and "head"? (pp.90-1)

ALL'OSPEDALE
At the hospital

It is useful to know a few basic phrases relating to hospitals for use in an emergency or in case you need to visit a friend or colleague in the hospital. Emergency rooms will treat all urgent cases free of charge, but citizens of non-EU countries will be asked to sign a payment declaration.

2 **Useful phrases** (5 minutes)

Familiarize yourself with these phrases. Conceal the Italian with the cover flap and test yourself.

Qual è l'orario di visita? *kwalay lorareeoh dee veezeetah*	What are the visiting hours?
Quanto ci vuole? *kwantoh chee vwolay*	How long does it take?
Farà male? *farah malay*	Will it hurt?
Si sdrai sul lettino. *see zdraee sool letteenoh*	Please lie down on the bed.
Non deve mangiare. *non devay manjaray*	You must not eat.
Non muova la testa. *non mwovah lah testah*	Don't move your head.
Apra la bocca. *aprah lah bokkah*	Open your mouth.
Deve fare le analisi del sangue. *devay faray lay analeezee del sangway*	You need a blood test.

Dov'è la sala d'aspetto?
dovay lah salah daspettoh
Where is the waiting room?

la flebo
lah flayboh
intravenous drip

Si sente meglio?
see sentay mellyoh
Are you feeling better?

3 Words to remember (4 minutes)

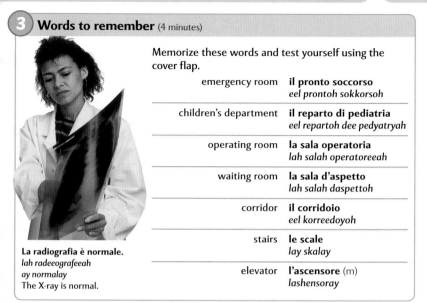

Memorize these words and test yourself using the cover flap.

emergency room	**il pronto soccorso** *eel prontoh sokkorsoh*
children's department	**il reparto di pediatria** *eel repartoh dee pedyatryah*
operating room	**la sala operatoria** *lah salah operatoreeah*
waiting room	**la sala d'aspetto** *lah salah daspettoh*
corridor	**il corridoio** *eel korreedoyoh*
stairs	**le scale** *lay skalay*
elevator	**l'ascensore** (m) *lashensoray*

La radiografia è normale.
lah radeeografeeah
ay normalay
The X-ray is normal.

4 Put into practice (3 minutes)

Join this conversation. Read the Italian on the left and follow the instructions to make your reply. Then test yourself by hiding the answers with the cover flap.

Forse c'è un'infezione.
forsay chay ooneenfetsyonay

You may have an infection.

Ask: Do I need tests?

Devo fare dei controlli?
devoh faray day kontrollee

Prima di tutto deve fare le analisi del sangue.
preemah dee toottoh devay faray lay analeezee del sangway

First you will need a blood test.

Ask: Will it hurt?

Farà male?
farah malay

5 Say it (2 minutes)

Does he need a blood test?

Where is the children's department?

Do I need an X-ray?

No, non si preoccupi.
noh, non see prayokkoopee

No, don't worry.

Ask: How long does it take?

Quanto ci vuole?
kwantoh chee vwolay

Risposte
Answers (Cover with flap)

RIPASSA E RIPETI
Review and repeat

1 The body

1 The body (4 minutes)

Name the numbered body parts in Italian.

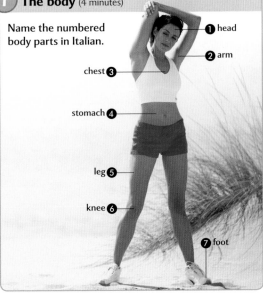

❶ head
❷ arm
chest ❸
stomach ❹
leg ❺
knee ❻
❼ foot

❶ la testa
lah testah

❷ il braccio
eel brachoh

❸ il petto
eel pettoh

❹ lo stomaco
loh stomakoh

❺ la gamba
lah gambah

❻ il ginocchio
eel jeenokkyoh

❼ il piede
eel pyeday

2 On the phone

2 On the phone (4 minutes)

You are arranging an appointment. Follow the conversation, replying in Italian following the English prompts.

Pronto? Tipografia Bartoli.
❶ I'd like to speak to Mr. Salvetti.

Chi parla, scusi?
❷ It's Dr. Pieri of Bonanni.

Mi dispiace, il signor Salvetti è in riunione.
❸ Can I leave a message?

Certo.
❹ The appointment is on Monday at 11 am.

Benissimo.
❺ Thank you, goodbye.

❶ Vorrei parlare con il signor Salvetti.
vorray parlaray kon eel seennyor salvettee

❷ Sono il dottor Pieri della Bonanni.
sonoh eel dottor pyayree dellah bonannee

❸ Posso lasciare un messaggio?
possoh lasharay oon messajjoh

❹ L'appuntamento è lunedì alle undici.
lappoontamentoh ay lunedee allay oondeechee

❺ Grazie, arrivederci.
gratseeay, arreevederchee

3 Clothing (3 minutes)

Say the Italian words for the numbered items of clothing.

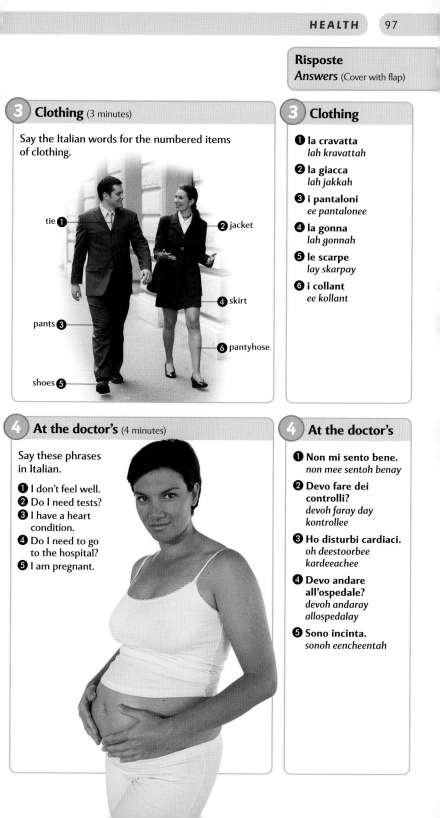

tie ❶
❷ jacket
❹ skirt
pants ❸
❻ pantyhose
shoes ❺

3 Clothing

❶ **la cravatta**
lah kravattah

❷ **la giacca**
lah jakkah

❸ **i pantaloni**
ee pantalonee

❹ **la gonna**
lah gonnah

❺ **le scarpe**
lay skarpay

❻ **i collant**
ee kollant

4 At the doctor's (4 minutes)

Say these phrases in Italian.

❶ I don't feel well.
❷ Do I need tests?
❸ I have a heart condition.
❹ Do I need to go to the hospital?
❺ I am pregnant.

4 At the doctor's

❶ **Non mi sento bene.**
non mee sentoh benay

❷ **Devo fare dei controlli?**
devoh faray day kontrollee

❸ **Ho disturbi cardiaci.**
oh deestoorbee kardeeachee

❹ **Devo andare all'ospedale?**
devoh andaray allospedalay

❺ **Sono incinta.**
sonoh eencheentah

GLI ALLOGGI
At home

Say the months of the year in Italian. (pp.28–9)

Ask "Is there an art gallery?" (pp.48–9) and "How many brothers do you have?" (pp.14–15)

The *apartment block* (**il palazzo**) is the most common form of urban housing in Italy. A single-*family house* (**la villetta**) is more common in rural areas. To find out the total number of rooms, you will need to ask "**Quante stanze?**". If you want to know how many bedrooms, ask "**Quante camere?**".

2 **Match and repeat** (5 minutes)

Match the numbered items to the list and test yourself using the cover flap.

1 **la finestra**
 lah feenestrah

2 **il muro**
 eel mooroh

3 **il comignolo**
 eel comeennyoloh

4 **il tetto**
 eel tettoh

5 **la grondaia**
 lah grondayah

6 **il viale**
 eel veealay

7 **la porta**
 lah portah

8 **le persiane**
 lay persyanay

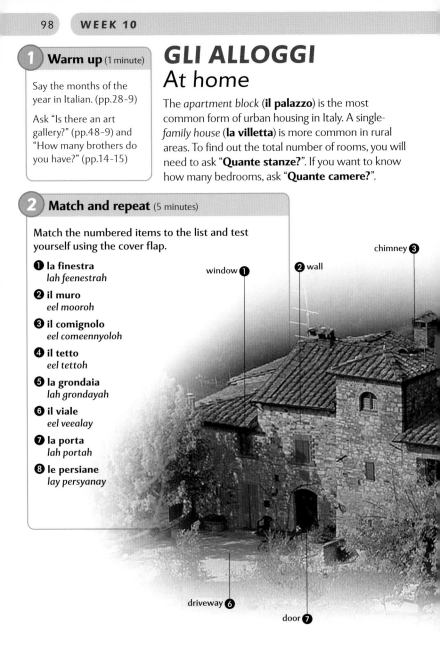

window **1**   **2** wall   chimney **3**

driveway **6**

door **7**

Cultural tip You almost never see an Italian home without shutters or roller shades at every window. These are closed at night and in the heat of the day. Curtains tend to be more for decoration. Most apartment blocks have at least one *balcony* (**il balcone**) for each apartment. These are often filled with plants to make up for the lack of a garden.

3 Words to remember (4 minutes)

Quant'è l'affitto al mese?
kwantay laffeettoh al mezay
What is the rent per month?

Familiarize yourself with these words and
test yourself using the cover flap.

room	**la stanza** *lah stantsah*
floor	**il pavimento** *eel paveementoh*
ceiling	**il soffitto** *eel soffeettoh*
bedroom	**la camera** *lah kamayrah*
bathroom	**il bagno** *eel bannyoh*
kitchen	**la cucina** *lah koocheenah*
dining room	**la sala da pranzo** *lah salah dah pranzoh*
living room	**il soggiorno** *eel sojjornoh*
basement	**la cantina** *lah kanteenah*
attic	**la soffitta** *lah soffeettah*

roof ❹   gutter ❺

shutters ❽

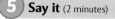

4 Useful phrases (3 minutes)

Learn these phrases and test yourself.

C'è il garage?
chay eel garadj

Is there a garage?

È libera subito?
ay leeberah soobeetoh

Is it available soon?

L'appartamento è ammobiliato?
appartamayntoh ay ammobeelyatoh

Is the flat furnished?

5 Say it (2 minutes)

Is there a dining room?

Is it large?

Is it available in July?

IN CASA
In the house

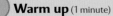

1 Warm up (1 minute)

What is the Italian for "table" (pp.20-1), "desk" (pp.80-1), "bed" (pp.60-1), and "restrooms"? (pp.52-3)

How do you say "soft," "beautiful," and "big"? (pp.64-5)

If you are renting accommodation in Italy, it is normal to be asked to pay for services such as electricity and heating on top of the rent; for short rentals of vacation flats or villas, they might be included in the rent. You may be asked to pay a *security deposit* (**versare una caparra** or **cauzione**).

2 Match and repeat (3 minutes)

Match the numbered items to the list in the panel on the left. Then test yourself by concealing the Italian with the cover flap.

❶ **il piano di lavoro**
eel peeanoh dee lavoroh

❷ **il lavello**
eel lavelloh

❸ **il forno a microonde**
eel fornoh ah meekrohonday

❹ **il forno**
eel fornoh

❺ **il fornello**
eel fornaylloh

❻ **il frigorifero**
eel freegoreeferoh

❼ **la sedia**
lah sedyah

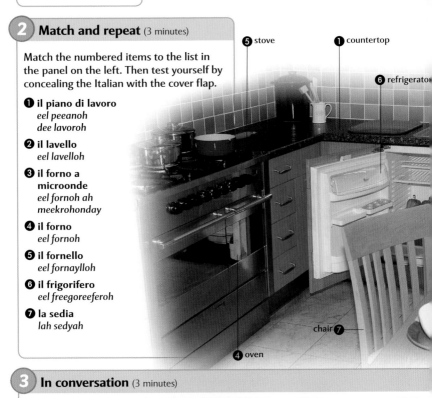

❺ stove ❶ countertop ❻ refrigerator chair ❼ ❹ oven

3 In conversation (3 minutes)

Questo è il forno.
kwestoh ay eel fornoh

This is the oven.

C'è anche la lavastoviglie?
chay ankay lah lavastoveellyay

Is there a dishwasher, too?

Sì, e il congelatore è grande.
see, ay eel konjelatoray ay granday

Yes, and there's a big freezer.

4 Words to remember (2 minutes)

Familiarize yourself with these words and test yourself using the flap.

Il divano è nuovo.
eel deevanoh ay nwovoh
The sofa is new.

❷ sink   microwave ❸

wardrobe	**l'armadio (m)** *larmadeeoh*	
armchair	**la poltrona** *lah poltronah*	
fireplace	**il caminetto** *eel kameenettoh*	
rug	**il tappeto** *eel tappaytoh*	
bathtub	**la vasca** *lah vaskah*	
toilet	**il bagno** *eel banyoh*	
bathroom sink	**il lavandino** *eel lavandeenoh*	
curtains	**le tende** *lay tenday*	

5 Useful phrases (4 minutes)

Learn these phrases and then test yourself using the cover flap to conceal the Italian.

The refrigerator is broken.	**Il frigorifero è rotto.** *eel freegoreeferoh ay rottoh*
The curtains are ugly.	**Le tende sono brutte.** *lay tenday sonoh broottay*
Is electricity included?	**La luce è inclusa?** *lah loochay ay eenkloosah*

6 Say it (2 minutes)

Is there a microwave?

I like the fireplace.

What a soft sofa!

Il lavello è nuovo.
eel lavelloh ay nwovoh

The sink is new.

E qui c'è la lavatrice.
ay kwee chay lah lavatreechay

And here's the washing machine.

Che belle piastrelle!
kay bellay piastrellay

What beautiful tiles!

IL GIARDINO
The backyard

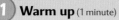

1 **Warm up** (1 minute)

What is the Italian for "day" and "month"? (pp.28-9)

Say the days of the week. (pp.28-9)

The yard of a house or villa may be communal, or at least partly shared. Check with the rental agent or travel agent. Not a traditional pastime among Italians, gardening for pleasure has become more popular in recent years. Garden nurseries stock a wide range of plants.

2 **Words to remember** (3 minutes)

Familiarize yourself with these words and test yourself using the cover flap.

il tosaerba *eel tozaerbah*	lawnmower
le cesoie *lay chezoyay*	shears
la vanga *lah vangah*	spade
il rastrello *eel rastrelloh*	rake
il vivaio *eel veevayoh*	garden nursery

terrace **1**

tree **2**

flowers **7**

8 weeds

soil **3**

path **9**

3 Useful phrases (4 minutes)

Learn these phrases and then test yourself using the cover flap.

The gardener comes once a week.	**Il giardiniere viene una volta alla settimana.** *eel jardeenyeray vyenay oonah voltah allah setteemanah*
Can you mow the lawn?	**Può tagliare l'erba?** *pwoh tallyaray lerbah*
Is the yard private?	**Il giardino è privato?** *eel jardeenoh ay preevatoh*
The yard needs watering.	**Bisogna annaffiare il giardino.** *beezonnyah annaffyaray eel jardeenoh*

5 hedge

4 lawn

4 Match and repeat (5 minutes)

Match the numbered items to the words in the panel on the right.

1 il patio
eel pateeoh

2 l'albero (m)
lalberoh

3 la terra
lah terrah

4 il prato
eel pratoh

5 la siepe
lah syepay

6 le piante
lay peeantay

7 i fiori
ee feeoree

8 le erbacce
lay erbacchay

9 il vialetto
eel vyalettoh

10 l'aiuola (f)
laywolah

6 plants

5 Say it (2 minutes)

The lawn needs water.

Are there any trees?

The gardener comes on Fridays.

10 flowerbed

GLI ANIMALI
Pets

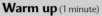

1 **Warm up** (1 minute)

Say "My name is John."
(pp.8–9)

Say "Don't worry."
(pp.94–5)

What's "your" in Italian?
(pp.12-13)

If you are considering taking your dog or other pet on an extended trip to Italy, discuss this with your veterinarian well before your departure date, and make sure you have the right documentation and vaccinations. Italy requires an Export Health Certificate.

2 **Match and repeat** (3 minutes)

Match the numbered animals to the Italian words in the panel on the left. Then test yourself using the cover flap.

1 **il gatto**
eel gattoh

2 **il coniglio**
eel koneellyoh

3 **l'uccello (m)**
loocchelloh

4 **il pesce**
eel peshay

5 **il cane**
eel kanay

6 **il criceto**
eel kreechetoh

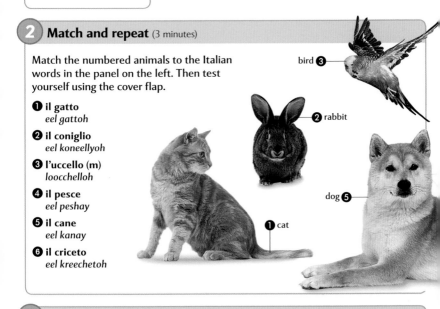

bird **3**

2 rabbit

dog **5**

1 cat

3 **Useful phrases** (4 minutes)

Learn these phrases and then test yourself using the cover flap.

Questo cane è buono? *kwestoh kanay ay bwonoh*	Is this dog friendly?
Posso portare il cane? *possoh portaray eel kanay*	Can I bring my dog?
Ho paura dei gatti. *oh paoorah day gattee*	I'm afraid of cats.
Il mio cane non morde. *eel mee-oh kanay non morday*	My dog doesn't bite.

Questo gatto ha le pulci.
kwestoh gattoh ah lay poolchee
This cat has fleas.

Cultural tip Many dogs in Italy are working dogs, and you may encounter them tethered or roaming free. Approach farms and rural houses with particular care, and keep away from the dog's territory. Look out for warning notices such as **Attenti al cane** (*Beware of the dog*).

ATTENTI AL CANE

4 Words to remember (4 minutes)

Familiarize yourself with these words and test yourself using the cover flap.

Il mio cane non sta bene.
eel mee-oh kanay non stah benay
My dog is not well.

vet	**il veterinario** *eel vetereenareeoh*
vaccination	**la vaccinazione** *lah vaccheenatsyonay*
pet passport	**il pet passport** *eel pet passport*
dog basket	**la cuccia** *lah koocchah*
cage	**la gabbia** *lah gabbyah*
dog bowl	**la ciotola del cane** *lah chotolah del kanay*
collar	**il collare** *eel kollaray*
leash	**il guinzaglio** *eel gweentsallyoh*
fleas	**le pulci** *lay poolchee*

6 hamster

fish **4**

5 Put into practice (3 minutes)

Join in this conversation. Read the Italian on the left and follow the instructions to make your reply. Then test yourself by concealing the answers with the cover flap.

È suo il cane?
ay soo-oh eel kanay

Is this your dog?

Say: Yes, he's called Sandy.

Sì, si chiama Sandy.
see, see keeamah sendee

Ho paura dei cani.
oh paoorah day kanee

I'm afraid of dogs.

Say: Don't worry. He's friendly.

Non si preoccupi. È buono.
non see preokkoopee. ay bwonoh

RIPASSA E RIPETI
Review and repeat

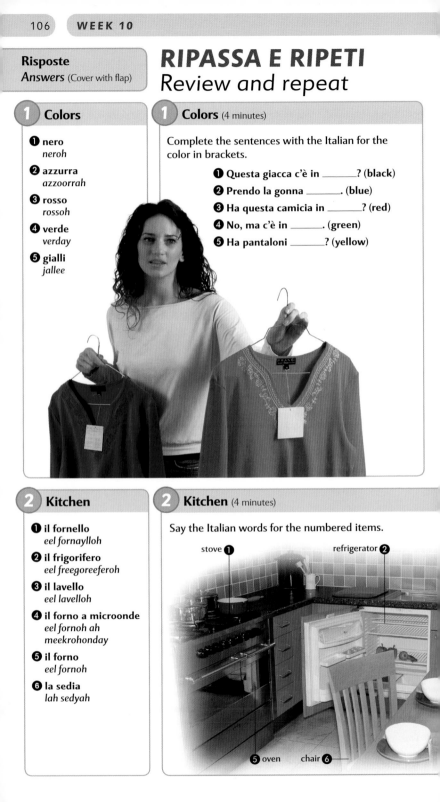

1 Colors

❶ **nero**
neroh

❷ **azzurra**
azzoorrah

❸ **rosso**
rossoh

❹ **verde**
verday

❺ **gialli**
jallee

1 Colors (4 minutes)

Complete the sentences with the Italian for the color in brackets.

❶ Questa giacca c'è in _____? (black)

❷ Prendo la gonna _____. (blue)

❸ Ha questa camicia in _____? (red)

❹ No, ma c'è in _____. (green)

❺ Ha pantaloni _____? (yellow)

2 Kitchen

❶ **il fornello**
eel fornaylloh

❷ **il frigorifero**
eel freegoreeferoh

❸ **il lavello**
eel lavelloh

❹ **il forno a microonde**
eel fornoh ah meekrohonday

❺ **il forno**
eel fornoh

❻ **la sedia**
lah sedyah

2 Kitchen (4 minutes)

Say the Italian words for the numbered items.

stove ❶   refrigerator ❷

❺ oven   chair ❻

3 House (4 minutes)

You are visiting a house in Italy. Join in the conversation, replying in Italian where you see the English prompts.

Questo è il soggiorno.
❶ What a lovely balcony!

E la cucina è molto bella.
❷ How many bedrooms?

Ci sono tre camere.
❸ Is there a garage?

No, ma c'è un giardino molto grande.
❹ Is the house available soon?

La casa è libera da luglio.
❺ What is the rent per month?

3 House

❶ **Che bel balcone!**
kay bel balkonay

❷ **Quante camere ci sono?**
kwantay kameray chee sonoh

❸ **C'è il garage?**
chay eel garadj

❹ **La casa è libera subito?**
lah kazah ay leeberah soobeetoh

❺ **Quant'è l'affitto al mese?**
kwantay laffeettoh al mezay

4 At home (3 minutes)

Say the Italian for the following items.

❶ washing machine
❷ sofa
❸ basement
❹ dining room
❺ tree
❻ garden

microwave ❹

❸ sink

4 At home

❶ **la lavatrice**
lah lavatreechay

❷ **il divano**
eel deevanoh

❸ **la cantina**
lah kanteenah

❹ **la sala da pranzo**
lah salah dah pranzoh

❺ **l'albero**
lalberoh

❻ **il giardino**
eel jardeenoh

1 Warm up (1 minute)

Ask "How do I get to the bank?", and "How do I get to the post office?" (pp.50-1 and pp.68-9)

What's the Italian for "passport"? (pp.54-5)

How do you ask "What time is it?" (pp.30-1)

LE POSTE E LA BANCA
Post office and bank

Cashpoints/ATMs are plentiful in Italy. In tourist resorts there are also bureaux de change (**il cambio**). Stamps are available from tobacconists (**il tabaccaio**) as well as post offices.

2 Words to remember: mail (3 minutes)

la busta *lah boostah*	envelope
il pacco *eel pakkoh*	package
via aerea *veeah a-ayreah*	by air mail
raccomandata *rakkomandatah*	registered mail
i francobolli *ee frankobollee*	stamps
il postino *eel posteenoh*	mail carrier
la cassetta delle lettere *lah kassettah dellay letteray*	mailbox

Familiarize yourself with these words and test yourself using the cover flap to conceal the Italian on the left.

la cartolina *lah kartoleenah* postcard

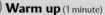

3 In conversation (3 minutes)

Vorrei prelevare dei soldi. *vorray prelevaray day soldee*

I'd like to withdraw some money.

Ha un documento d'identità? *ah oon dokoomentoh deedenteetah*

Do you have any identification?

Sì, ecco il mio passaporto. *see, ekkoh eel mee-oh passaportoh*

Yes, here's my passport.

4 Words to remember: bank (2 minutes)

Familiarize yourself with these words and test yourself using the cover flap to conceal the Italian on the right.

Come posso pagare?
komay possoh pagaray
How can I pay?

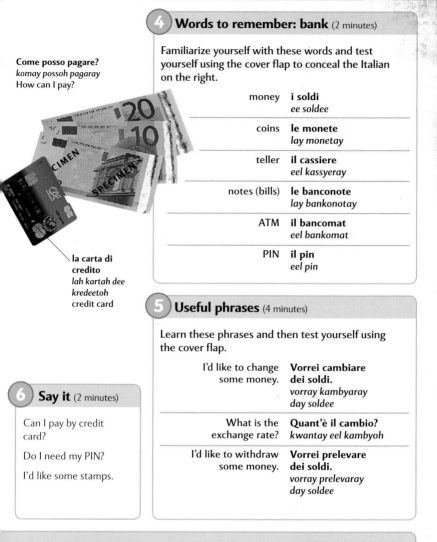

money	**i soldi**	*ee soldee*
coins	**le monete**	*lay monetay*
teller	**il cassiere**	*eel kassyeray*
notes (bills)	**le banconote**	*lay bankonotay*
ATM	**il bancomat**	*eel bankomat*
PIN	**il pin**	*eel pin*

la carta di credito
lah kartah dee kredeetoh
credit card

5 Useful phrases (4 minutes)

Learn these phrases and then test yourself using the cover flap.

I'd like to change some money.	**Vorrei cambiare dei soldi.** *vorray kambyaray day soldee*
What is the exchange rate?	**Quant'è il cambio?** *kwantay eel kambyoh*
I'd like to withdraw some money.	**Vorrei prelevare dei soldi.** *vorray prelevaray day soldee*

6 Say it (2 minutes)

Can I pay by credit card?

Do I need my PIN?

I'd like some stamps.

Può battere il pin.
pwoh battayray eel pin

Please type in your PIN.

Devo anche firmare?
devoh ankay feermaray

Do I need to sign, too?

No, non è necessario.
noh, non ay nechessaryoh

No, that's not necessary.

1 Warm up (1 minute)

What is the Italian for "doesn't work"? (pp.60-1)

What's the Italian for "today" and "tomorrow"? (pp.28-9)

RIPARAZIONI
Repairs

You can combine the Italian words on these pages with the vocabulary you learned in week 10 to help you explain basic problems and cope with arranging most repairs. When setting up building work or a repair, it's a good idea to agree on the price and method of payment in advance.

2 Words to remember (4 minutes)

Familiarize yourself with these words and test yourself using the cover flap.

l'idraulico *leedraooleekoh*	plumber
l'elettricista *lelettreecheestah*	electrician
il meccanico *eel mekkaneekoh*	mechanic
il muratore *eel mooratoray*	handyman
l'imbianchino *leembyankeenoh*	decorator
il falegname *eel falennyamay*	carpenter
il tecnico *eel tayneekoh*	technician
la donna delle pulizie *lah donnah dellay pooleetsyay*	cleaner

la chiave
lah keeavay
tire iron

Non ho bisogno di un meccanico.
non oh beezonnyoh dee oon mekkaneekoh
I don't need a mechanic.

3 In conversation (3 minutes)

La lavatrice non funziona.
lah lavatreechay non foontsyonah

The washing machine is not working.

Sì, il tubo è rotto.
see, eel tooboh ay rottoh

Yes, the hose is broken.

Può ripararlo?
pwoh reepararloh

Can you repair it?

4 Useful phrases (3 minutes)

Learn these phrases and then test yourself using the cover flap.

Please clean the bathroom.	**Può pulire il bagno?** *pwoh pooleeray eel bannyoh*
Can you repair the boiler?	**Può riparare la caldaia?** *pwoh reepararay lah kaldayah*
Do you know a good electrician?	**Conosce un bravo elettricista?** *konoshay oon bravoh elettreecheestah*

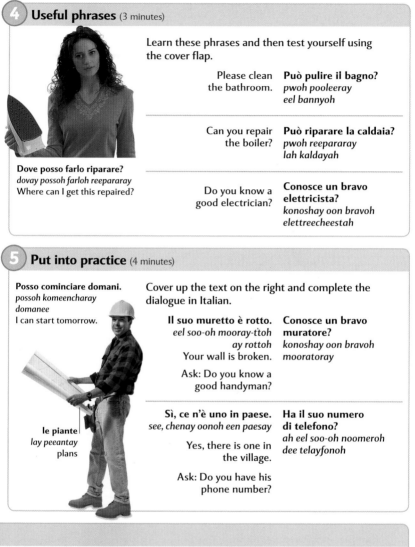

Dove posso farlo riparare?
dovay possoh farloh reepararay
Where can I get this repaired?

5 Put into practice (4 minutes)

Posso cominciare domani.
possoh komeencharay domanee
I can start tomorrow.

Cover up the text on the right and complete the dialogue in Italian.

le piante
lay peeantay
plans

Il suo muretto è rotto. *eel soo-oh mooray-ttoh ay rottoh* Your wall is broken. Ask: Do you know a good handyman?	**Conosce un bravo muratore?** *konoshay oon bravoh mooratoray*
Sì, ce n'è uno in paese. *see, chenay oonoh een paesay* Yes, there is one in the village. Ask: Do you have his phone number?	**Ha il suo numero di telefono?** *ah eel soo-oh noomeroh dee telayfonoh*

No, deve cambiarlo.
noh, devay kambeearloh

No, you need to change it.

Può farlo oggi?
pwoh farloh ojjee

Can you do it today?

No, torno domani.
noh, tornoh domanee

No, I'll come back tomorrow.

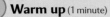
VENIRE
To come

The verb **venire** (*to come*) is a very common verb that can be used to make a variety of useful idiomatic expressions. Remember that in Italian, the sense of continuing action is implied in the simple present tense—for example, **vengo** can mean both *I come* and *I am coming*.

2 **Venire: to come** (6 minutes)

Say the different forms of **venire** (*to come*) aloud. Use the cover flap to test yourself and, when you are confident, practice the sample sentences below.

(io) vengo *(ee-oh) vengoh*	I come
(tu) vieni *(too) vyenee*	you come (informal singular)
(lei) viene *(lay) vyenay*	you come (formal singular)
(lui/lei) viene *(loo-ee/lay) vyenay*	he/she/it comes
(noi) veniamo *(noy) veneeamoh*	we come
(voi) venite *(voy) veneetay*	you come (plural)
(loro) vengono *(loroh) vengonoh*	they come
Veniamo tutte le estati. *veneeamoh toottay lay estatee*	We come every summer.
Vengo anch'io. *vengoh ankeeoh*	I am coming, too.
Vengono in treno. *vengonoh een trenoh*	They are coming by train.

Lei viene dalla Nigeria.
lay vyenay dallah neejayreeah
She comes from Nigeria.

Conversational tip Note that when in English you say *come and see* in Italian this translates as **vieni a vedere** (*come to see*). In the same way, *Shall I come and pick you up?* translated in Italian is **Vengo a prenderti?**.

3 Useful phrases (4 minutes)

Learn these phrases and then test yourself using the cover flap.

When can I come?	**Quando posso venire?** *kwandoh possoh veneeray*
Come and see.	**Vieni a vedere.** *vyenee ah vederay*
The cleaner comes every Monday.	**La donna delle pulizie viene il lunedì.** *lah donnah dellay pooleetsyay vyenay eel loonedee*
Come with me. (informal/formal)	**Vieni/venga con me.** *vyenee/vengah kon may*

Venite alla mia festa?
veneetay allah mee-ah festah
Are you coming to my party?

4 Put into practice (4 minutes)

Join in this conversation. Read the Italian on the left and follow the instructions to make your reply. Then test yourself by concealing the answers with the cover flap.

Buongiorno. Parrucchiere Leo.
bwonjornoh. parrookkyeray layo

Hello, this is Leo's hair salon.

Say: I'd like an appointment.

Vorrei un appuntamento.
vorray oon appoontamentoh

Quando vuol venire?
kwando vwol veneeray

When do you want to come?

Say: Can I come today?

Posso venire oggi?
possoh veneeray ojjee

Sì certo, a che ora?
see chertoh, a kay orah

Yes, of course. What time?

Say: At 10:30.

Alle dieci e mezzo.
allay deeaychee ay metsoh

Warm up (1 minute)

What's the Italian for "big/tall" and "small/short"? (pp.64–5)

Say "The room is big" and "The bed is small." (pp.64–5)

LA POLIZIA E IL CRIMINE
Police and crime

In an emergency, you can contact the police by dialing 112. You may have to explain your problem in Italian, so some basic vocabulary is useful. In the event of a burglary, the police will usually come to the house.

Words to remember: crime (4 minutes)

Familiarize yourself with these words.

il furto *eel foortoh*	burglary
il rapporto di polizia *eel rapportoh dee poleetseeah*	police report
il ladro *eel ladroh*	thief
la denuncia *lah denoonchah*	statement
il/la testimone *eel/lah testeemonay*	witness
l'avvocato *lavvokatoh*	lawyer

Voglio un avvocato.
vollyoh oonavvokatoh
I want a lawyer.

Useful phrases (3 minutes)

Learn these phrases and then test yourself using the cover flap.

Sono stato/a derubato/a. *sonoh statoh/ah deroobatoh/ah*	I've been robbed.
Cosa hanno rubato? *kozah annoh roobatoh*	What was stolen?
Ha visto chi è stato? *ah veestoh kee ay statoh*	Did you see who did it?
Quando è successo? *kwandoh ay succhessoh*	When did it happen?

gli oggetti di valore
lly ojjayttee dee valoray
valuables

4 Words to remember: appearance (5 minutes)

Learn these words. Remember some adjectives have a feminine form.

man/men	**l'uomo/gli uomini**
	lwomoh/lly womeenee
woman/women	**la donna/le donne**
	lah donnah/lay donnay
tall	**alto/alta**
	altoh/altah
short	**basso/bassa**
	bassoh/bassah
young	**giovane**
	jovanay
old	**vecchio/vecchia**
	vekkyoh/vekkyah
fat	**grasso/grassa**
	grassoh/grassah
thin	**magro/magra**
	magroh/magrah
beard	**la barba**
	lah barbah
glasses	**gli occhiali**
	lly okkyalee
long/short hair	**i capelli lunghi/corti**
	ee kapellee loongee/kortee

Ha i capelli scuri e i baffi.
ah ee kapellee skooree ay ee baffee
He has dark hair and a mustache.

Ha i capelli neri corti.
ah ee kapellee neree kortee
He has short, black hair.

Cultural tip If you are affected by a crime or other emergency in Italy, you can go to the **Carabinieri**, a force that is part of the army and operates even in small towns. Call them by dialing 112.

---

5 Put into practice (2 minutes)

Practice these phrases. Then use the cover flap to conceal the text on the right and follow the instructions to make your reply in Italian.

Lo può descrivere?   **Basso e grasso.**
loh pwoh deskreeveray   *bassoh ay grassoh*

Can you describe him?

Say: Short and fat.

E i capelli?   **Capelli lunghi e barba.**
ay ee kapellee   *kapellee loongee ay barbah*

And the hair?

Say: Long hair and a beard.

Risposte
Answers (Cover with flap)

RIPASSA E RIPETI
Review and repeat

1 To come

❶ **vengo**
vengoh

❷ **viene**
vyenay

❸ **veniamo**
veneeamoh

❹ **venite**
veneetay

❺ **vengono**
vengonoh

1 To come (3 minutes)

Fill in the blanks with the correct form of **venire** (*to come*).

❶ (io) _____ alle quattro.

❷ Il giardiniere _____ una volta alla settimana.

❸ (noi) _____ in treno.

❹ (voi) _____ con noi?

❺ I miei genitori _____ lunedì.

2 Bank and mail

❶ **la carta di credito**
lah cartah dee kredeetoh

❷ **le banconote**
lay bankonotay

❸ **il pacco**
eel pakkoh

❹ **i francobolli**
ee frankobollee

❺ **la cartolina**
lah kartoleenah

2 Bank and mail (4 minutes)

Name the numbered items in Italian.

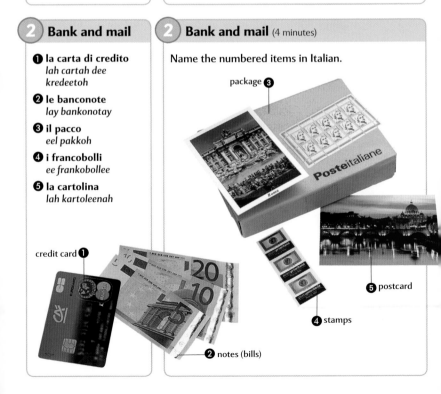

package ❸

credit card ❶

❺ postcard

❹ stamps

❷ notes (bills)

3 Appearance (4 minutes)

What do these descriptions mean?

❶ **Un uomo alto e magro.**

❷ **Una donna con i capelli corti e gli occhiali.**

❸ **Sono bassa e ho i capelli lunghi.**

❹ **È vecchia e grassa.**

❺ **Lui ha gli occhi azzurri e la barba.**

3 Appearance

❶ A tall, thin man.

❷ A woman with short hair and glasses.

❸ I'm short and I have long hair.

❹ She is old and fat.

❺ He has blue eyes and a beard.

4 The pharmacy (4 minutes)

You are asking a pharmacist for advice. Join in the conversation, replying in Italian where you see the English prompts.

Buongiorno, dica?
❶ I have a cough.

Ha anche il raffreddore?
❷ No, but I have a headache.

Prenda queste pastiglie.
❸ Do you have that as a syrup?

Certo. Ecco lo sciroppo.
❹ Thank you. How much is that?

Nove euro.
❺ Here you are. Goodbye.

4 The pharmacy

❶ **Ho la tosse.**
oh lah tossay

❷ **No, ma ho mal di testa.**
noh, mah oh mal dee testah

❸ **Le ha in sciroppo?**
lay ah een sheeroppoh

❹ **Grazie. Quant'è?**
gratseeay. kwantay

❺ **Ecco. Arrivederci.**
ekkoh. arreevederchee

IL TEMPO LIBERO
Leisure time

Italy, with its long history and rich culture, provides numerous opportunities for cultural pursuits, as well as modern leisure activities. Many Italians are interested in the arts and spend the weekends in *historic cities* (**città d'arte**) or, when the weather is warm, at the seaside.

1 Warm up (1 minute)

What is the Italian for "museum" and "art gallery"? (pp.48-9)

Say "What beautiful curtains!" (pp.100-01)

Ask "Do you want...?" informally. (p.22-3)

2 Words to remember (4 minutes)

Familiarize yourself with these words and test yourself using the cover flap to conceal the Italian on the left.

Amo l'opera.
amoh lopayrah
I love opera.

gli spettatori
lly spettatoree
audience

il teatro *eel tayatroh*	theater
il cinema *eel cheenemah*	movie theater
la discoteca *lah diskotekah*	discotheque
la musica *lah moozeekah*	music
l'arte (f) *lartay*	art
lo sport *loh sport*	sports
viaggiare *veeajjaray*	traveling
i videogiochi *ee veedayohjokkee*	video games

3 In conversation (4 minutes)

Vuoi giocare a tennis?
vwoee jokaray ah tennees

Do you want to play tennis?

No, lo sport non mi piace.
noh, loh sport non mee peeachay

No, I don't like sports.

Cosa fai nel tempo libero?
kozah faee nel tempoh leeberoh

What do you do in your free time?

Detesto i videogiochi.
detestoh ee veedayohjokkee
I hate video games.

la galleria
lah galereeah
balcony

la platea
lah platayah
orchestra

4 Useful phrases (4 minutes)

Learn these phrases and then test yourself using the cover flap.

What do you do (formal/informal) in your spare time?	**Cosa fa/fai nel tempo libero?** *kozah fah/faee nel tempoh leeberoh*
I like the theater.	**Mi piace il teatro.** *mee peeachay eel teatroh*
I prefer the movies.	**Io preferisco il cinema.** *ee-oh preferisko eel cheenemah*
I'm interested in art.	**Mi interessa l'arte.** *mee eenteressah lartay*
That's boring!	**Che noia!** *kay noeeah*

5 Say it (2 minutes)

I'm interested in music.

I prefer sports.

I don't like opera.

Mi piace lo shopping.
mee peeachay loh shoppeen

I like shopping.

Detesto lo shopping.
Detestoh loh shoppeen

I hate shopping.

Non c'è problema, vado da sola.
non chay problemah, vadoh dah solah

No problem, I'll go on my own.

LO SPORT E GLI HOBBY
Sport and hobbies

1 **Warm up** (1 minute)

Ask "Do you (formal) want to play tennis?" (pp.22-3, pp.118-19)

Say "I like the theater" and "I prefer traveling." (pp.118-19)

Say "That doesn't interest me." (pp.118-19)

The verb **fare** (to do) is useful for talking about hobbies. With sports you can also use **giocare** (to play)—for example, **gioco a tennis** (I play tennis). **Fare** is also used to describe the weather, as in **fa freddo** (it's cold).

2 **Words to remember** (3 minutes)

Memorize these words and then test yourself.

il calcio *eel kalchoh*	soccer
il rugby *eel regbee*	rugby
il tennis *eel tennees*	tennis
il nuoto *eel nwotoh*	swimming
la vela *lah velah*	sailing
la pesca *lah peskah*	fishing
la pittura *lah peettoorah*	painting
la palestra *lah palestrah*	gymnastics

il bunker
eel bunker
bunker

il golfista
eel golfeestah
golfer

Gioco a golf tutti i giorni.
jokoh ah golf toottee ee jornee
I play golf every day.

3 **Useful phrases** (4 minutes)

Familiarize yourself with these phrases.

Gioco a rugby. *jokoh ah regbee*	I play rugby.
Gioca a tennis. *jokah ah tennees*	He plays tennis.
Fa un corso di pittura. *fah oon korsoh dee peettoorah*	She is on a painting course.

4) Fare: to do or to make (4 minutes)

Fa caldo oggi.
fah kaldoh ojjee
It's hot today.

____ **la bandierina**
lah bandeeayreenah
flag

____ **il campo da golf**
eel kampoh dah golf
golf course

The verb **fare** (*to do* or *to make*) is also used to describe the weather. Learn its different forms and practice the sample sentences below.

I do	**(io) faccio** *(ee-oh) facchoh*
you do (informal singular)	**(tu) fai** *(too) faee*
you do (formal singular)	**(lei) fa** *(lay) fah*
he/she/it does	**(lui/lei) fa** *(loo-ee/lay) fah*
we do	**(noi) facciamo** *(noy) facchamoh*
you do (plural)	**(voi) fate** *(voy) fatay*
they do	**(loro) fanno** *(loroh) fannoh*
What do you do? (formal/informal)	**Cosa fai/fate?** *kozah faee/fatay*
I go hiking.	**Faccio escursionismo.** *facchoh ayskursyoneesmoh*

5) Put into practice (3 minutes)

Learn these phrases. Then cover the text on the right and complete the dialogue in Italian. Check your answers.

Cosa ti piace fare?
kozah tee peeachay faray
What do you like doing?

Say: I like playing tennis.

Mi piace giocare a tennis.
mee peeachay jokaray ah tennees

Giochi anche a calcio?
jokee anchay ah kalchoh
Do you play soccer, too?

Say: No. I play rugby.

No. Gioco a rugby.
noh. jokoh ah regbee

Quando giochi?
kwandoh jokee
When do you play?

Say: I play every week.

Gioco tutte le settimane.
jokoh toottay lay setteemanay

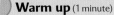

RAPPORTI SOCIALI
Socializing

Say "my husband" and "my wife." (pp.12-13)

How do you say "lunch" and "dinner" in Italian? (pp.20-1)

Say "Sorry, I'm busy." (pp.32-3)

The Italian dinner table is the center of the social world; you can expect to do a lot of socializing while enjoying food and wine. It is best to use the more polite **Lei** form at first to talk to people you meet socially; when they start to call you **tu**, you can reciprocate.

2 **Useful phrases** (3 minutes)

l'ospite
lospeetay
guest

Learn these phrases and then test yourself.

Vuol venire a cena con me? *vwol veneeray ah chenah con may*	Would you like to come to dinner with me?
È libero/a mercoledì prossimo? *ay leeberoh/ah merkoledee prosseemoh*	Are you free next Wednesday?
Magari un'altra volta. *magaree oonaltrah voltah*	Perhaps another time.

Cultural tip When you go to someone's house for the first time, it is polite to bring flowers, chocolate, or a bottle of good wine. If you are invited again, having seen your host's house, you can bring something a little more personal.

3 **In conversation** (3 minutes)

Vuol venire a cena da me martedì?
vwol veneeray ah chenah dah may martedee

Would you like to come to dinner on Tuesday?

Mi dispiace, martedì non posso.
mee deespeeachay, martedee non possoh

I'm sorry, I can't on Tuesday.

Facciamo giovedì?
facchamoh jovedee

What about Thursday?

la padrona di casa
lah padronah dee kazah
hostess

4 **Words to remember** (3 minutes)

Familiarize yourself with these words and test
yourself using the cover flap.

party	**la festa** *lah festah*
dinner party	**la cena** *lah chenah*
invitation	**l'invito (m)** *leenveetoh*
reception	**il rinfresco** *eel reenfreskoh*
gift	**il regalo** *eel regaloh*

5 **Put into practice** (5 minutes)

Join in this conversation.

**Facciamo una festa
sabato. Siete liberi?**
*facchamoh oonah festah
sabatoh. seeaytay leeberee*

We're having a party on
Saturday. Are you free?

Say: Yes, how nice!

Sì, che bello!
see, kay belloh

Benissimo.
beneesseemoh

That's great.

Ask: What time does
it start?

A che ora comincia?
ah kay orah komeenchah

Grazie dell'invito.
gratseeay delleenveetoh
Thank you for inviting us.

Benissimo.
beneesseemoh

That's great.

Porti suo marito.
portee soo-oh mareetoh

Please bring your husband.

Grazie. A che ora?
gratseeay. ah kay orah

Thank you. What time?

Risposte
Answers (Cover with flap)

RIPASSA E RIPETI
Review and repeat

1 Animals

❶ **il pesce**
eel peshay

❷ **l'uccello**
loocchelloh

❸ **il coniglio**
eel koneellyoh

❹ **il gatto**
eel gattoh

❺ **il criceto**
eel kreechetoh

❻ **il cane**
eel kanay

1 Animals (3 minutes)

Name the numbered animals in Italian.

rabbit ❸

❶ fish

hamster ❺

❹ cat

2 I like...

❶ **Mi piace il rugby.**
mee peeachay eel regbee

❷ **Non mi piace il golf.**
non mee peeachay eel golf

❸ **Mi piace la pittura.**
mee peeachay lah peettoorah

2 I like... (4 minutes)

Say the following in Italian:

❶ I like rugby.
❷ I don't like golf.
❸ I like to paint.

❶

❷

❸

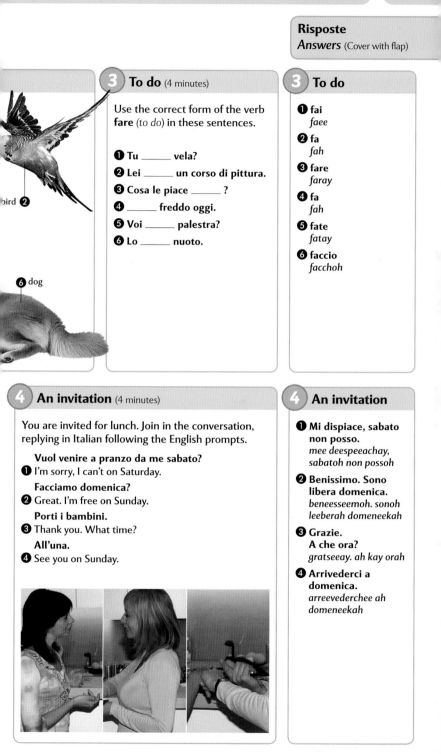

bird ❷

❻ dog

3 To do (4 minutes)

Use the correct form of the verb **fare** *(to do)* in these sentences.

❶ Tu _____ vela?

❷ Lei _____ un corso di pittura.

❸ Cosa le piace _____ ?

❹ _____ freddo oggi.

❺ Voi _____ palestra?

❻ Lo _____ nuoto.

3 To do

❶ **fai**
faee

❷ **fa**
fah

❸ **fare**
faray

❹ **fa**
fah

❺ **fate**
fatay

❻ **faccio**
facchoh

4 An invitation (4 minutes)

You are invited for lunch. Join in the conversation, replying in Italian following the English prompts.

Vuol venire a pranzo da me sabato?
❶ I'm sorry, I can't on Saturday.

Facciamo domenica?
❷ Great. I'm free on Sunday.

Porti i bambini.
❸ Thank you. What time?

All'una.
❹ See you on Sunday.

4 An invitation

❶ **Mi dispiace, sabato non posso.**
mee deespeeachay, sabatoh non possoh

❷ **Benissimo. Sono libera domenica.**
beneesseemoh. sonoh leeberah domeneekah

❸ **Grazie. A che ora?**
gratseeay. ah kay orah

❹ **Arrivederci a domenica.**
arreevederchee ah domeneekah

Reinforce and progress

Regular practice is the key to maintaining and advancing your language skills. In this section you will find a variety of suggestions for reinforcing and extending your knowledge of Italian. Many involve returning to exercises in the book and using the dictionaries to extend their scope. Go back through the lessons in a different order, mix and match activities to make up your own 15-minute daily program, or focus on topics that are of particular relevance to your current needs.

1 Warm up (1 minute)

How do you say "he is" and "they are"? (pp.14–15)

Now say "he is not" and "they are not." (pp.14–15)

What is Italian for "my mother"? (pp.10–11)

Keep warmed up
Revisit the Warm Up boxes to remind yourself of key words and phrases. Make sure you work your way through all of them on a regular basis.

3 I'd like... (3 minutes)

Say "I'd like" the following:

4 sugar   **1** black coffee   croissant **3**

cappuccino **2**

Review and repeat again
Work through a Review and Repeat lesson as a way of reinforcing words and phrases presented in the course. Return to the main lesson for any topic on which you are no longer confident.

3 In conversation: taxi (2 minutes)

Carry on conversing
Reread the In Conversation panels. Say both parts of the conversation, paying attention to the pronunciation. Where possible, try incorporating new words from the dictionary.

Al mercato di San Lorenzo, per favore.
al merkatoh dee san lorentsoh, per favoray

Benissimo, signore.
beneesseemoh, seennyoray

Very well, sir.

Mi lasci qui, per favore.
mee lashee kwee, per favoray

Can you drop me here, please?

3 Useful phrases (5 minutes)

Learn these phrases and then test yourself using the cover flap.

The room is too cold/hot.	**In camera fa troppo freddo/caldo.** *een kamayrah fah troppoh freddoh/kaldoh*
There are no towels.	**Non ci sono gli asciugamani.** *non chee sonoh lly ashugamanee*
I'd like some soap.	**Vorrei del sapone.** *vorray del saponay*
The shower doesn't work very well.	**La doccia non funziona bene.** *lah docchah non funtseeonah benay*

Practice phrases
Return to the Useful Phrases and Put into Practice exercises. Test yourself using the cover flap. When you are confident, devise your own versions of the phrases, using new words from the dictionary.

Match, repeat, and extend

Remind yourself of words related to specific topics by returning to the Match and Repeat and Words to Remember exercises. Test yourself using the cover flap. Discover new words in that area by referring to the dictionary and menu guide.

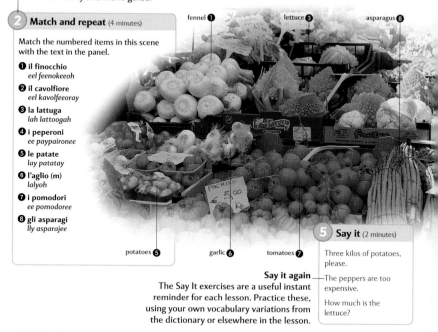

2 Match and repeat (4 minutes)

Match the numbered items in this scene with the text in the panel.

1 il finocchio
eel feenokeeoh

2 il cavolfiore
eel kavolfeeoray

3 la lattuga
lah lattoogah

4 i peperoni
ee paypaironee

5 le patate
lay patatay

6 l'aglio (m)
lalyoh

7 i pomodori
ee pomodoree

8 gli asparagi
lly asparajee

fennel **1**   lettuce **3**   asparagus **8**

potatoes **5**   garlic **6**   tomatoes **7**

5 Say it (2 minutes)

Three kilos of potatoes, please.

The peppers are too expensive.

How much is the lettuce?

Say it again
The Say It exercises are a useful instant reminder for each lesson. Practice these, using your own vocabulary variations from the dictionary or elsewhere in the lesson.

Using other resources

In addition to working with this book, try the following language extension ideas:

Visit Italy and try out your new skills with native speakers. Or find out if there is an Italian community near you. There may be shops, cafés, restaurants, and clubs. Try to visit some of these and use your Italian to order food and drink and strike up conversations. Most native speakers will be happy to speak Italian to you.

Join a language class or club. There are usually evening and day classes available at a variety of different levels. Or you could start a club yourself if you have friends who are also interested in keeping up their Italian.

Look at Italian magazines and newspapers. The pictures will help you to understand the text. Advertisements are also a useful way of expanding your vocabulary.

Use the Internet, where you can find all kinds of websites for learning languages, some of which offer free online help and activities. You can also find Italian websites for anything from renting a house to shampooing your pet. You can even access Italian radio and TV stations online. Start by going to an Italian search engine, such as *iltrovatore.it*, and typing in a hobby or sport that interests you, or set yourself a challenge, such as finding a two-bedroom apartment for rent in Florence.

MENU GUIDE

This guide lists the most common terms you may encounter on Italian menus or when shopping for food. If you can't find an exact phrase, try looking up its component parts.

A

abbacchio alla romana Roman-style spring lamb
acciughe sott'olio anchovies in oil
aceto vinegar
acqua water
acqua minerale gassata sparkling mineral water
acqua minerale non gassata still mineral water
acqua naturale still mineral water, tap water
affettato misto variety of cold, sliced meats
affogato al caffè hot espresso on ice cream
aglio garlic
agnello lamb
albicocche apricots
al forno roast
amatriciana chopped bacon and tomato sauce
ananas pineapple
anatra duck
anatra all'arancia duck in orange sauce
anguilla in umido stewed eel
anguria watermelon
antipasti appetizers
antipasti misti mixed appetizers
aperitivo aperitif
aragosta lobster
arancia orange
aranciata orangeade
aringa herring
arista di maiale al forno roast chine of pork
arrosto roast
arrosto di tacchino roast turkey
asparagi asparagus
avocado all'agro avocado with dressing

B

baccalà dried cod
baccalà alla vicentina Vicentine-style dried cod
bagnacauda vegetables (often raw) in a sauce of oil, garlic, and anchovy

Barbaresco dry red wine from Piedmont
Barbera dry red wine from Piedmont
Bardolino dry red wine from the Veneto region
Barolo dark, dry red wine from Piedmont
basilico basil
bavarese ice-cream cake with cream
bel paese soft, white cheese
besciamella white sauce
bignè cream puff
birra beer
birra chiara light beer, lager
birra grande large beer
birra piccola small beer
birra scura dark beer
bistecca ai ferri grilled steak
bistecca (di manzo) steak
bolognese ground beef and tomato sauce
braciola di maiale pork steak
branzino al forno baked sea bass
brasato braised beef with herbs
bresaola dried, salted beef eaten with oil and lemon
brioche type of croissant
brodo clear broth
brodo di pollo chicken broth
brodo vegetale clear vegetable broth
budino pudding
burro butter
burro di acciughe anchovy butter

C

caciotta tender, white cheese from Central Italy
caffè coffee
caffè corretto espresso with a dash of liqueur
caffè latte half coffee, half hot milk
caffè lungo weak espresso
caffè macchiato espresso with a dash of milk
caffè ristretto strong espresso

calamari in umido stewed squid
calamaro squid
calzone folded pizza with tomato and cheese
camomilla chamomile tea
cannella cinnamon
cannelloni al forno baked egg pasta rolls stuffed with meat
cappuccino espresso with foaming milk sprinkled with cocoa powder
capretto al forno roast kid
carbonara sauce of egg, bacon, and cheese
carciofi artichokes
carciofini sott'olio baby artichokes in oil
carne meat
carote carrots
carpaccio finely sliced beef fillets with oil, lemon, and parmesan
carré di maiale al forno roast pork loin
cassata siciliana ice-cream cake with chocolate, glacé fruit, and ricotta
castagne chestnuts
cavoletti di Bruxelles Brussels sprouts
cavolfiore cauliflower
cavolo cabbage
cefalo mullet
cernia grouper (fish)
charlotte ice-cream cake with cream, cookies, and fruit
Chianti dark red Tuscan wine
cicoria chicory
cicorino small chicory plants
ciliege cherries
cime di rapa sprouting broccoli
cioccolata chocolate
cioccolata calda hot chocolate
cipolle onions
cocktail di gamberetti shrimp cocktail
conchiglie alla marchigiana pasta shells in tomato sauce with ham, celery, carrot, and parsley
coniglio rabbit

coniglio in umido *stewed rabbit*

consommé *clear meat or chicken broth*

contorni *vegetables*

coperto *cover charge*

coppa *cured neck of pork*

costata alla fiorentina *T-bone veal steak*

costata di manzo *T-bone beef steak*

cotechino *spiced pork sausage for boiling*

cotoletta *veal, pork, or lamb chop*

cotoletta ai ferri *grilled veal or pork chop*

cotoletta alla milanese *veal chop in breadcrumbs*

cotoletta alla valdostana *veal chop with ham and cheese, in breadcrumbs*

cotolette di agnello *lamb chops*

cotolette di maiale *pork chops*

cozze *mussels*

cozze alla marinara *mussels in white wine*

crema *custard dessert made with eggs and milk*

crema al caffè *coffee custard dessert*

crema al cioccolato *chocolate custard dessert*

crema di funghi *cream of mushroom soup*

crema di piselli *cream of pea soup*

crema pasticciera *confectioner's custard*

crêpes Suzette *crepes flambéed with orange sauce*

crescente *fried bread made with flour, lard, and eggs*

crespelle *savory crepe*

crostata di frutta *fruit tart*

D, E

dadi *bouillon cubes*

datteri *dates*

degustazione *tasting*

degustazione di vini *wine tasting*

dentice al forno *baked dentex (type of sea bream)*

digestivo *dessert liqueur*

dolci *sweets, desserts, cakes*

endivia belga *white chicory*

entrecôte (di manzo) *beef entrecote*

espresso *strong, black coffee*

F

fagiano *pheasant*

fagioli *beans*

fagioli borlotti in umido *borlotti (kidney beans) in sauce of tomato, vegetables, and herbs*

fagiolini *long, green beans*

faraona *guinea fowl*

fegato *liver*

fegato alla veneta *liver in butter with onions*

fegato con salvia e burro *liver in butter and sage*

fettuccine *ribbon-shaped pasta*

fichi *figs*

filetti di pesce persico *fillets of perch*

filetti di sogliola *fillets of sole*

filetto ai ferri *grilled fillet of beef*

filetto al cognac *fillet of beef flambé*

filetto al pepe verde *fillet of beef with green peppercorns*

filetto al sangue *rare fillet of beef*

filetto ben cotto *well-done fillet of beef*

filetto (di manzo) *fillet of beef*

filetto medio *medium-cooked fillet of beef*

finocchi gratinati *fennel au gratin*

finocchio *fennel*

fonduta *cheese fondue*

formaggi misti *variety of cheeses*

fragole *strawberries*

fragole con gelato/ panna *strawberries and ice cream/cream*

frappé *fruit or milk shake with crushed ice*

Frascati *dry white wine from area around Rome*

frittata *type of omelet*

frittata alle erbe *herb omelet*

fritto misto *mixed seafood in batter*

frittura di pesce *variety of fried fish*

frutta *fruit*

frutta alla fiamma *fruit flambé*

frutta secca *dried nuts and raisins*

frutti di bosco *mixture of strawberries, raspberries, mulberries, etc.*

frutti di mare *seafood*

funghi *mushrooms*

funghi trifolati *mushrooms fried in garlic and parsley*

G

gamberetti *shrimp*

gamberi *large shrimp*

gamberoni *jumbo shrimp*

gazzosa *clear lemonade*

gelatina *gelatin*

gelato *ice cream*

gelato di crema *vanilla-flavored ice cream*

gelato di frutta *fruit-flavored ice cream*

gnocchetti verdi agli spinaci e al gorgonzola *small flour, potato, and spinach dumplings with melted gorgonzola*

gnocchi *small flour and potato dumplings*

gnocchi alla romana *small milk and semolina dumplings with butter*

Gorgonzola *strong blue cheese from Lombardy*

grancevola *spiny spider crab*

granchio *crab*

granita *crushed ice drink*

grigliata di pesce *grilled fish*

grigliata mista *mixed grill (meat or fish)*

grissini *thin, crisp breadsticks*

gruviera *Gruyère cheese*

I

indivia *endive*

insalata *salad*

insalata caprese *salad of tomatoes and mozzarella*

insalata di funghi porcini *boletus mushroom salad*

insalata di mare *seafood salad*

insalata di nervetti *boiled beef or veal served cold with beans and pickles*

insalata di pomodori *tomato salad*

insalata di riso *rice salad*

insalata mista *mixed salad*

insalata russa *Russian salad (diced cooked vegetables in mayonnaise)*

insalata verde *green salad*

involtini *meat rolls stuffed with ham and herbs*

L

lamponi *raspberries*

lasagne al forno *meat lasagna with cheese*

latte *milk*

latte macchiato con cioccolato *hot milk sprinkled with cocoa*

lattuga *lettuce*
leggero *light*
legumi *legumes (beans)*
lemonsoda *sparkling lemon drink*
lenticchie *lentils*
lepre *hare*
limonata *lemon-flavored soda*
limone *lemon*
lingua *tongue*

M

macedonia di frutta *fruit salad*
maiale *pork*
maionese *mayonnaise*
mandarino *mandarin*
mandorla *almond*
manzo *beef*
marroni *chestnuts*
Marsala *fortified wine*
marzapane *marzipan*
mascarpone *soft, mild cheese*
medaglioni di vitello *veal medallions*
mela *apple*
melanzane *eggplant*
melone *melon*
menta *mint*
meringata *meringue pie*
merluzzo *cod*
merluzzo alla pizzaiola *cod in tomato sauce with anchovies and capers*
merluzzo in bianco *cod with oil and lemon*
messicani in gelatina *rolls of veal in gelatin*
millefoglie *pastry layered with custard*
minestra in brodo *noodle soup*
minestrone *vegetable soup with rice or pasta*
mirtilli *bilberries*
more *mulberries or blackberries*
moscato *sweet wine*
mousse al cioccolato *chocolate mousse*
mozzarella *buffalo cheese*
mozzarella in carrozza *fried slices of bread and mozzarella*

N, O

nasello *hake*
nocciole *hazelnuts*
noce moscata *nutmeg*
noci *walnuts*
nodino *veal chop*
olio *oil*
origano *oregano*
osso buco *stewed shin of veal*
ostriche *oysters*

P

paglia e fieno *mixed plain and green tagliatelle*
paillard di manzo *slices of grilled beef*
paillard di vitello *slices of grilled veal*
pane *bread*
panino *filled roll*
panna *cream*
parmigiana di melanzane *eggplant baked with cheese*
pasta al forno *pasta baked in white sauce and grated cheese*
pasta e fagioli *thick soup with puréed borlotti beans and pasta rings*
pasta e piselli *pasta with peas*
pasticcio di fegato d'oca *baked pasta dish with goose liver*
pasticcio di lepre *baked pasta dish with hare*
pasticcio di maccheroni *baked macaroni*
pastina in brodo *noodle soup*
patate *potatoes*
patate al forno/arrosto *roast potatoes*
patate fritte *french fries*
patate in insalata *potato salad*
pecorino *strong, hard sheep's milk cheese*
penne *pasta quills*
penne ai quattro formaggi *pasta with four-cheese sauce*
penne all'arrabbiata *pasta with tomato and chili pepper sauce*
penne panna e prosciutto *pasta with cream and ham sauce*
pepe *pepper (spice)*
peperoncino *crushed chili pepper*
peperoni *peppers*
peperoni ripieni *stuffed peppers*
peperoni sott'olio *peppers in oil*
pera *pear*
pesca *peach*
pesce *fish*
pesce al cartoccio *fish baked in foil with herbs*
pesce in carpione *marinaded fish*
pesto *sauce of basil, pine nuts, Parmesan, garlic, and oil*
pinot *dry white wine from the Veneto region*
pinzimonio *raw vegetables with oil and vinegar*
piselli *peas*

piselli al prosciutto *broth with peas, ham, and basil*
pizzaiola *slices of cooked beef in tomato sauce, oregano, and anchovies*
pizzoccheri alla Valtellinese *pasta strips with vegetables and cheese*
polenta *boiled cornmeal left to set and sliced*
polenta e osei *polenta with small birds*
polenta pasticciata *layers of polenta, tomato sauce, and cheese*
pollo *chicken*
pollo alla cacciatora *chicken in white wine and mushroom sauce*
pollo alla diavola *deep-fried chicken pieces*
polpette *meatballs*
polpettone *meatloaf*
pomodori *tomatoes*
pomodori ripieni *stuffed tomatoes*
pompelmo *grapefruit*
porri *leeks*
prezzemolo *parsley*
primi piatti *first courses*
prosciutto cotto *cooked ham*
prosciutto crudo *type of cured ham*
prugne *plums*
punte di asparagi all'agro *asparagus tips in oil and lemon*
purè di patate *mashed potatoes*
puttanesca *tomato sauce with anchovies, capers, and black olives*

Q, R

quaglie *quails*
radicchio *chicory*
ragù *meat-based sauce*
rapanelli *radishes*
ravioli *stuffed pasta parcels*
ravioli al pomodoro *meat ravioli in tomato sauce*
razza *skate*
ricotta *ricotta cheese*
risi e bisi *risotto with peas and ham*
riso *rice*
risotto *rice cooked in stock*
risotto alla castellana *risotto with mushroom, ham, cream, and cheese*
risotto alla milanese *risotto with saffron*
risotto al nero di seppia *risotto with cuttlefish ink*
risotto al tartufo *truffle risotto*

roast-beef all'inglese *thinly sliced cold roast beef*

robiola *type of soft cheese from Lombardy*

rognone trifolato *kidney in garlic, oil, and parsley*

rosatello/rosato *rosé wine*

rosmarino *rosemary*

S

salame *salami*

sale *salt*

salmone affumicato *smoked salmon*

salsa cocktail/rosa *mayonnaise and ketchup sauce for fish and seafood*

salsa di pomodoro *tomato sauce*

salsa tartara *tartar sauce*

salsa vellutata *white sauce made with clear broth instead of milk*

salsa verde *sauce for meat, with parsley and oil*

salsiccia *sausage*

salsiccia di cinghiale *wild boar sausage*

salsiccia di maiale *pork sausage*

saltimbocca alla romana *slices of veal stuffed with ham and sage and fried*

salvia *sage*

sambuca (con la mosca) *aniseed-flavor liqueur served with a coffee bean*

sarde ai ferri *grilled sardines*

scaloppine *veal escalopes*

scaloppine al prezzemolo *veal escalopes with parsley*

scamorza alla griglia *grilled soft cheese*

scampi alla griglia *grilled shrimp*

secco *dry*

secondi piatti *second courses, main courses*

sedano *celery*

selvaggina *game*

semifreddo *dessert of ice cream and sponge cakes*

senape *mustard*

seppie in umido *stewed cuttlefish*

servizio compreso *service charge included*

servizio escluso *service charge excluded*

Soave *dry white wine from the Veneto region*

sogliola *sole*

sogliola ai ferri *grilled sole*

sogliola al burro *sole cooked in butter*

sogliola alla mugnaia *sole cooked in flour and butter*

sorbetto *sorbet, soft ice cream*

soufflé al formaggio *cheese soufflé*

soufflé al prosciutto *ham soufflé*

speck *cured, smoked ham*

spezzatino di vitello *veal stew*

spiedini *assorted chunks of spit-cooked meat or fish*

spinaci *spinach*

spinaci all'agro *spinach with oil and lemon*

spremuta di ... *freshly squeezed ... juice*

spumante *sparkling wine*

stracchino *soft cheese from Lombardy*

stracciatella *soup of beaten eggs in clear broth*

strudel di mele *apple strudel*

succo di ... *... juice*

sugo al tonno *tomato sauce with garlic, tuna, and parsley*

T

tacchino ripieno *stuffed turkey*

tagliata *finely cut beef fillet cooked in the oven*

tagliatelle *thin pasta strips*

tagliatelle rosse *tagliatelle with chopped red peppers*

tagliatelle verdi *tagliatelle with spinach*

tagliolini *thin soup noodles*

tartine *small sandwiches*

tartufo *ice cream covered in cocoa or chocolate; truffle*

tè *tea*

tiramisù *dessert with coffee-soaked sponge, Marsala, mascarpone, and cocoa powder*

tonno *tuna*

torta *tart, flan*

torta di ricotta *type of cheesecake*

torta salata *savory quiche*

tortellini *pasta shapes filled with minced pork, ham, Parmesan, and nutmeg*

trancio di palombo *smooth dogfish steak*

trancio di pesce spada *swordfish steak*

trenette col pesto *flat spaghetti with pesto sauce*

triglie *mullet (fish)*

trippa *tripe*

trota *trout*

trota affumicata *smoked trout*

trota al burro *trout cooked in butter*

trota alle mandorle *trout with almonds*

trota bollita *boiled trout*

U

uccelletti *small birds wrapped in bacon, served on cocktail sticks*

uova *eggs*

uova alla coque *boiled eggs*

uova al tegamino con pancetta *fried eggs and bacon*

uova farcite *eggs with tuna, capers, and mayonnaise filling*

uova sode *hard-boiled eggs*

uva *grapes*

uva bianca *white grapes*

uva nera *black grapes*

V

vellutata di asparagi *creamed asparagus with egg yolks*

vellutata di piselli *creamed peas with egg yolks*

verdura *vegetables*

vermicelli *very fine, thin pasta, often used in soups*

vino *wine*

vino bianco *white wine*

vino da dessert *dessert wine*

vino da pasto *table wine*

vino da tavola *table wine*

vino rosso *red wine*

vitello *veal*

vitello tonnato *cold sliced veal in tuna, anchovy, oil, and lemon sauce*

vongole *clams*

W, Z

würstel *hot dog*

zabaglione *creamy dessert of eggs, sugar, and Marsala*

zafferano *saffron*

zucca *pumpkin*

zucchine *zucchini*

zucchine al pomodoro *zucchini in tomato, garlic, and parsley sauce*

zucchine ripiene *stuffed zucchini*

zuccotto *ice-cream cake with sponge cake, cream, and chocolate*

zuppa *soup*

zuppa di cipolle *onion soup*

zuppa di cozze *mussel soup*

zuppa di lenticchie *lentil soup*

zuppa di pesce *fish soup*

DICTIONARY
English to Italian

The gender of an Italian noun is indicated by the word for *the*: **il** or **lo** (masculine), **la** (feminine), and their plural forms **i** or **gli** (masculine) and **le** (feminine). When **lo** or **la** are abbreviated to **l'** in front of a vowel or **h**, then the gender is indicated by the abbreviations (m) or (f). Italian adjectives (adj) vary according to the gender and number of the word they describe, and the masculine form is shown here. In general, adjectives that end in **-o** adopt an **-a** ending in the feminine form, and those that end in **-e** usually stay the same. Plural endings are **-i** for masculine and **-e** for feminine.

A

a **un/uno/una/un'**
about: about 16 **circa 16;**
   a book about Venice **un libro su Venezia**
accelerator **l'acceleratore** (m)
accident **l'incidente** (m)
accommodation **l'alloggio** (m), **il posto**
accountant **il ragioniere/ la ragioniera**
ache **il dolore**
adapter **il riduttore**
address **l'indirizzo** (m)
admission charge **il prezzo d'ingresso**
advance (on payment) **il anticipo;** *in advance* **anticipato**
after **dopo**
afternoon **il pomeriggio**
aftershave **il dopobarba**
again **di nuovo**
against **contro**
agenda **l'ordine del giorno** (m)
AIDS **l'Aids** (f)
air **l'aria** (f)
air conditioning **l'aria condizionata** (f)
aircraft **l'aereo** (m)
airline **la linea aerea**
air mail **via aerea**
air mattress **il materassino gonfiabile**
airport **l'aeroporto** (m)
airport bus **l'autobus navetta** (m)
aisle (in supermarket, etc.) **la fila**
alarm clock **la sveglia**
alcohol **l'alcol** (m)
all **tutto;** *all the streets* **tutte le strade;** *that's all* **questo è tutto**
allergic **allergico**
allowed **permesso**
almost **quasi**

alone **solo**
Alps **le Alpi**
already **già**
always **sempre**
am: I am **(io) sono**
ambulance **l'ambulanza** (f)
America **l'America** (f)
American **americano**
and **e**
ankle **la caviglia**
anniversary **il anniversario**
another **un altro, un'altra**
answering machine **la segreteria telefonica**
antique shop **l'antiquario** (m)
antiseptic **l'antisettico** (m)
apartment **l'appartamento** (m)
aperitif **l'aperitivo** (m)
appetite **l'appetito** (m)
appetizers **i primi piatti**
apple **la mela**
application form **il modulo per la domanda**
appointment **l'appuntamento** (m)
apricot **l'albicocca** (f)
April **aprile**
architecture **l'architettura** (f)
are: you are (singular, formal) **(Lei) è;** *(singular, informal)* **(tu) sei;** *(plural)* **(voi) siete;** *we are* **(noi) siamo;** *they are* **(loro) sono**
arm **il braccio**
armchair **la poltrona**
arrange (appointment, etc.) **fissare**
arrivals **gli arrivi**
arrive **arrivare**
art **l'arte** (f)
art gallery **la pinacoteca, la galleria d'arte**
artist **l'artista** (m/f)
as: as soon as possible **(il) più presto possibile**
ashtray **il portacenere**
asparagus **gli asparagi**

aspirin **l'aspirina** (f)
asthmatic **asmatico**
at: at the post office **all'ufficio postale;** *at night* **di notte;** *at 3 o'clock* **alle tre**
athletic shoes **le scarpe da ginnastica**
ATM **il bancomat**
attic **la soffitta**
attractive **attraente**
audience **gli spettatori**
August **agosto**
aunt **la zia**
Australia **l'Australia** (f)
Australian **australiano (-a)**
automatic **automatico**
fall **l'autunno** (m)
away: is it far away? **è l. ontano?;** *go away!* **vattene!**
awful **terribile, orribile**

B

baby **il bambino/ la bambina**
baby carriage **la carrozzina**
back (not front) **la parte posteriore;** *(body)* **la schiena;** *to come back* **tornare**
backpack **lo zaino**
bacon **la pancetta**
bad **cattivo**
bag **la borsa, il sacchetto**
baggage claim **il ritiro bagagli**
bait **l'esca** (f)
bake **cuocere (al forno)**
bakery **la pasticceria**
balcony **il balcone;** *(in theater)* **la galleria**
ball (soccer, etc.) **la palla, il pallone;** *(tennis, etc.)* **la pallina**
banana **la banana**
band (musicians) **la banda**
bandage **la fascia;** *(adhesive)* **il cerotto**

bank **la banca**
banknote **la banconota**
bar (drinks) **il bar;** bar of chocolate **la tavoletta di cioccolata**
barbecue **il barbecue;** (occasion) **la grigliata all'aperto**
barber shop **il barbiere**
bargain **l'affare** (m)
basement **il seminterrato**
basket **il cestino;** (in supermarket) **il cestello**
bath: to take a bath fare **il bagno**
bathroom **il bagno**
bathtub **la vasca**
bathroom **il bagno**
battery **la batteria**
be (verb) **essere**
beach **la spiaggia**
beans **i fagioli**
beard **la barba**
beautiful **bello**
because **perché**
bed **il letto**
bed linen **le lenzuola**
bedroom **la camera (da letto)**
bedspread **il copriletto**
beef **il manzo**
beer **la birra**
before ... **prima di ...**
beginner **il/la principiante**
beginners' slope **la discesa per principianti**
behind **dietro;** behind ... **dietro a ...**
beige **beige**
bell (church) **la campana;** (door) **il campanello**
below **sotto**
belt **la cintura**
beside ... **vicino a ...**
best **il migliore**
better (than) **migliore (di)**
between ... **fra ...**
bicycle **la bicicletta**
big **grande**
bikini **il bikini**
bird **l'uccello** (m)
birthday **il compleanno;** happy birthday! **buon compleanno!**
bite (by dog) **il morso;** (by insect) **la puntura;** (verb: by dog) **mordere;** (verb: by insect) **pungere**
bitter **amaro**
black **nero**
black currant **il ribes nero**

blanket **la coperta**
bleach **la varecchina;** (verb: hair) **ossigenare**
blind (cannot see) **cieco;** (on window) **la tenda avvolgibile**
blond (adj) **biondo/bionda**
blood **il sangue;** blood test **le analisi del sangue**
blouse **la camicetta**
blue **azzurro;** (navy blue) **blu**
boarding pass **la carta d'imbarco**
boat **la nave;** (small) **la barca;** (passenger) **il battello**
body **il corpo**
boil (verb: of water) **bollire;** (egg, etc.) **far bollire**
boiled **lesso**
boiler **la caldaia**
bolt (on door) **il catenaccio;** (verb) **chiudere con il catenaccio**
bone **l'osso** (m); (fish) **la lisca**
book **il libro;** (verb) **prenotare**
booking office **la biglietteria**
bookstore **la libreria**
boot **lo stivale**
border **il confine**
boring **noioso;** that's boring! **che noia!**
born **nato;** I was born in 1965 **sono nato nel 1965;** I was born in London **sono nato a Londra**
both of them **tutti e due;** both ... and ... **sia ... che ...**
bottle **la bottiglia**
bottle opener **l'apribottiglie** (m)
bottom **il fondo;** at the bottom (of) **in fondo (a)**
bowl **la scodella, la ciotola;** (mixing bowl) **la terrina**
box **la scatola;** (of wood, etc.) **la cassetta**
box office **il botteghino**
boy **il ragazzo**
bra **il reggiseno**
bracelet **il braccialetto**
brake **il freno;** (verb) **frenare**
branch (of company) **la filiale**
bread **il pane**
bread shop **la panetteria**
breakdown (car) **il guasto;** (nervous) **l'esaurimento nervoso** (m)
breakfast **la colazione**
breathe **respirare**
bridge **il ponte**

briefcase **la cartella**
bring **portare**
British **britannico**
brochure **l'opuscolo** (m)
broken **rotto;** broken leg **la gamba rotta**
brooch **la spilla**
brother **il fratello**
brown **marrone**
bruise **il livido**
brush (hair) **la spazzola;** (paint) **il pennello;** (cleaning) **la scopa;** (verb: hair) **spazzolare**
bucket **il secchio**
budget **il budget**
building **l'edificio** (m)
bumper **il paraurti**
bunker (golf) **il bunker**
burglar **il ladro**
burglary **il furto**
burn **la bruciatura;** (verb) **bruciare**
bus **l'autobus** (m); (long-distance) **il pullman**
business **l'affare** (m); it's none of your business **non sono affari tuoi;** business card **il biglietto da visita**
bus station **la stazione degli autobus**
bus stop **la fermata dell'autobus**
busy (occupied) **occupato;** (telephone) **occupato;** (bar, etc.) **animato**
but **ma**
butcher shop **la macelleria**
butter **il burro**
button **il bottone**
buy **comprare**
by: by the window **vicino alla finestra;** by Friday **entro venerdì;** by myself **da solo;** written by ... **scritto da ...**

C

cabbage **il cavolo**
cable car **la funivia**
café **il caffè, il bar**
cage **la gabbia**
cake **la torta**
calculator **il calcolatore**
call **la chiamata;** what's it called? **come si chiama?**
camera **la macchina fotografica**
camper trailer **la roulotte**
camper van **il camper**
campfire **il falò**

campground **il campeggio**

camshaft **l'albero a camme** (m)

can (vessel) **la lattina;** (verb: to be able) can I have ...? **posso avere ...?;** can you ...? **potreste ...?**

Canada **il Canada**

Canadian **canadese**

canal **il canale**

candle **la candela**

canoe **la canoa**

can opener **l'apriscatole** (m)

cap (bottle) **il tappo;** (hat) **il berretto**

car **l'auto** (m)**, la macchina**

carburetor **il carburatore**

card (greetings card) **il biglietto di auguri;** playing cards **le carte da gioco**

careful **attento;** be careful! **stia attento!**

caretaker **il portinaio/ la portinaia**

carpenter **il falegname**

carpet **il tappeto**

carrot **la carota**

carry out (verb) **da portare via**

car seat (for a baby) **il seggiolino per macchina**

cart **il carrello**

case (suitcase) **la valigia**

cash **il denaro, gli spicci;** (verb) **riscuotere;** to pay cash **pagare in contanti**

cashier **il cassiere**

cassette **la cassetta**

cassette player **il mangianastri**

castle **il castello**

cat **il gatto**

cathedral **il duomo, la cattedrale**

Catholic **cattolico**

cauliflower **il cavolfiore**

cave **la grotta**

CD **il compact disc**

ceiling **il soffitto**

cellar **la cantina**

cell phone **il cellulare, il telefonino**

cemetery **il cimitero**

central heating **il riscaldamento centrale**

center **il centro**

certificate **il certificato**

certo **certainly**

chair **la sedia;** swivel chair **la sedia girevole**

change (money) **il cambio, gli spicci;** (verb: money, trains) **cambiare;** (clothes) **cambiarsi**

charger **il caricabatterie**

cheap **economico, a buon mercato**

check **l'assegno** (m)**;** (restaurant) **il conto**

checkbook **il libretto degli assegni**

check in (verb) **fare il check-in**

check-in **il check-in;** check-in desk **lo sportello del check-in**

check-out **la cassa**

cheers! (toast) **alla salute!, cin cin!**

cheese **il formaggio**

cherry **la ciliegia**

chess **gli scacchi**

chest (part of body) **il petto;** (furniture) **il baule**

chest of drawers **il cassettone**

chewing gum **il chewing-gum**

chicken **il pollo**

child **il bambino;** (female) **la bambina**

children **i bambini;** (own children) **i figli;** children's ward **il reparto di pediatria**

chimney **il comignolo**

china **la porcellana**

chips **le patatine**

chocolate **la cioccolata;** box of chocolates **la scatola di cioccolatini**

chop (food) **la costoletta;** (verb) **tagliare (a pezzetti)**

Christmas **il Natale**

church **la chiesa**

cigar **il sigaro**

cigarette **la sigaretta**

city **la città**

class **la classe**

classical music **la musica classica**

clean (adj) **pulito;** (verb) **pulire**

cleaner **la donna delle pulizie**

clear (obvious) **chiaro;** (water) **limpido**

clever **bravo, intelligente**

client **il cliente**

clock **l'orologio** (m)

close (near) **vicino (a)** (verb) **chiudere**

closed **chiuso**

clothes **i vestiti**

clothespin **la molletta**

clubs (cards) **i fiori**

clutch **la frizione**

coat hanger **l'attaccapanni** (m)

coat **il capotto**

coffee **il caffè**

coin **la moneta**

cold (illness) **il raffreddore;** (adj) **freddo;** I have a cold **ho un raffreddore**

collar **il colletto;** (for dog) **il collare**

colleague **il collega**

collection (stamps, etc.) **la collezione**

color **il colore**

color film **il rullino a colori**

comb **il pettine;** (verb) **pettinare**

come **venire;** I come from ... **sono di ...;** come here! (formal/informal) **vieni/ venga qui!;** come with me (formal/informal) **vieni/ venga con me**

comforter **il piumino**

compartment **lo scompartimento**

complicated **complicato**

computer **il computer;** computer games **i videogiochi**

concert **il concerto**

conditioner (hair) **il balsamo**

condom **il preservativo**

conductor (bus) **il bigliettaio;** (orchestra) **il direttore**

conference **la conferenza;** conference room **la sala conferenze**

congratulations! **congratulazioni!**

connection **la coincidenza**

consulate **il consolato**

contact lenses **le lenti a contatto**

contraceptive **il contraccettivo**

contract **il contratto**

cook **il cuoco/la cuoca,** (verb) **cucinare**

cookie **il biscotto**

cool **fresco**

cork **il tappo**

corkscrew **il cavatappi**

corner **l'angolo** (m)

corridor **il corridoio**

cosmetics **i cosmetici**

cost (verb) **costare;** what does it cost? **quanto costa?**

cotton **il cotone**

cotton balls **il cotone idrofilo**

cough **la tosse;** (verb) **tossire**

countertop **il piano di lavoro**

country (state) **il paese;** (not town) **la campagna**

course (educational) **il corso**
cousin **il cugino/la cugina**
crab **il granchio**
cramp **il crampo**
crayfish **il gambero**
crazy **pazzo**
cream (dairy) **la crema, la panna**; (lotion) **la crema**
credit card **la carta di credito**
crew **l'equipaggio** (m)
crib **il lettino**
croissant **la brioche**
crowded **affollato**
cruise **la crociera**
crutches **le stampelle**
cry (to weep) **piangere**; (to shout) **gridare**
cucumber **il cetriolo**
cufflinks **i gemelli**
cup **la tazza**
cupboard **l'armadio** (m)
curlers **i bigodini**
curls **i ricci**
curtain **la tenda**
cushion **il cuscino**
customs **la dogana**
cut **il taglio**; (verb) **tagliare**

D

dad **il papà, il babbo**
dairy **la latteria**; dairy products **i latticini**
damp **umido**
dance **il ballo**; (verb) **ballare**
dangerous **pericoloso**
dark **scuro**
daughter **la figlia**
day **il giorno**
dead **morto**
deaf **sordo**
dear **caro**
debit card **la carta assegni**
December **dicembre**
deck (of cards) **il mazzo di carte**
decorator **l'imbianchino**
deep **profondo**
degree: I have a degree in ... **sono laureato in ...**
delayed **in ritardo**
deliberately **deliberatamente**
delicatessen **la salumeria**
delivery **la consegna**
dentist **il/la dentista**
dentures **la dentiera**
deodorant **il deodorante**
department **il reparto**
department store **il grande magazzino**

departure **la partenza**; departures **le partenze**; departure lounge **la sala d'attesa**
designer **il grafico/la grafica**
desk **la scrivania**
desserts **i dessert**
develop (film) **sviluppare**
diabetic **diabetico**
diamond (jewel) **il diamante**
diamonds (cards) **i quadri**
diapers **i pannolini**
diarrhea **la diarrea**
dictionary **il dizionario**
die **morire**
diesel **il gasolio**
different **diverso**; that's different! **è diverso!**; I'd like a different one **ne vorrei un altro**
difficult **difficile**
dining room **la sala da pranzo**
dinner **la cena**
directory (telephone) **la guida telefonica**
dirty **sporco**
disabled (people) **i disabili**
discount **la riduzione**
discount rate **la tariffa ridotta**
dishtowel **lo strofinaccio**
dishwasher **la lavastoviglie**
dishwashing liquid **il detersivo per i piatti**
dive **il tuffo**; (verb) **tuffarsi**
diving board **il trampolino**
divorced **divorziato**
do **fare**; how do you do? **piacere di conoscerla**; what do you do? **che lavoro fa?**
dock **il molo**
doctor (academic) **il dottore/la dottoressa**; (medical) **il medico**
document **il documento**
dog **il cane**; dog basket **la cuccia**; dog bowl **la ciotola del cane**
doll **la bambola**
dollar **il dollaro**
door **la porta**; (of car) **lo sportello**
double room **la matrimoniale, la camera doppia**
doughnut **il krapfen**
down **giù**
downtown **il centro città**
drawer **il cassetto**
dress **il vestito**

drink **la bibita**; (verb) **bere**; would you like a drink? **vorresti qualcosa da bere?**
drinking water **l'acqua potabile** (f)
drive (verb) **guidare**
driver **il guidatore/la guidatrice**; (of bus, truck, etc.) **l'autista** (m/f)
driver's license **la patente (di guida)**
driveway **il viale**
drops **le gocce**
drunk **ubriaco**
dry **asciutto**; (wine) **secco**
dry-cleaner's **la lavanderia a secco**
during **durante**
duster **lo straccio per la polvere**

E

each (every) **ogni**; twenty euros each **venti euro ciascuno**
ear **l'orecchio** (m); ears **le orecchie**
early **presto**; see you soon **a presto**
earphones **gli auricolari**
earrings **gli orecchini**
east **l'est** (m)
easy **facile**
eat **mangiare**
egg **l'uovo** (m)
eight **otto**
eighteen **diciotto**
eighty **ottanta**
either: either of them **l'uno o l'altro**
elastic **elastico**
elbow **il gomito**
electric **elettrico**; electrical hookup **la presa di corrente**
electrician **il/la elettricista**
electricity **l'elettricità** (f)
elevator **l'ascensore** (m)
eleven **undici**
else: something else **qualcos'altro**; someone else **qualcun'altro**; somewhere else **da qualche altra parte**
email **l'email** (f), **la posta elettronica**
email address **l'indirizzo di posta elettronica** (m)
embarrassing **imbarazzante**
embassy **l'ambasciata** (f)
emergency **l'emergenza** (f)

emergency exit **l'uscita di sicurezza** (f)
emergency department **il pronto soccorso**
empty **vuoto**
end **la fine**
engaged (to be married) **fidanzato/fidanzata**
engine (car) **il motore;** (train) **la locomotiva**
engineering **l'ingegneria**
England **l'Inghilterra** (f)
English **inglese**
enlargement **l'ampliamento** (m)
enough **abbastanza**
entrance **l'entrata** (f)
envelope **la busta**
epileptic **epilettico**
eraser **la gomma**
escalator **la scala mobile**
especially **particolarmente**
estimate **il preventivo**
evening **la sera**
every **ogni;** *every day* **tutti i giorni**
everyone **ognuno, tutti**
everything **tutto**
everywhere **dappertutto**
example **l'esempio** (m); *for example* **per esempio**
excellent **ottimo, eccellente**
excess baggage **il bagaglio in eccesso**
exchange (verb) **scambiare**
exchange rate **il (tasso di) cambio**
excursion **l'escursione** (f)
excuse me! (to get past) **permesso!;** (to get attention) **mi scusi!;** (when sneezing, etc.) **scusate!**
executive **il dirigente**
exhaust (car) **la marmitta**
exhibition **la mostra**
exit **l'uscita** (f)
expensive **caro, costoso**
expressway **l'autostrada** (f)
extension cord **la prolunga**
eye **l'occhio** (m); *eyes* **gli occhi**
eyebrow **il sopracciglio**

F

face **la faccia**
faint (unclear) **indistinto;** (verb) **svenire**
fair (funfair) **il luna park;** (trade) **la fiera (commerciale);** *it's not fair* **non è giusto**
false teeth **la dentiera**
family **la famiglia**
fan (ventilator) **il ventilatore;** (enthusiast) **l'ammiratore** (m)
fan belt **la cinghia della ventola**
fantastic **fantastico**
far **lontano;** *how far is it to ...?* **quanto dista da qui ...?**
fare **il biglietto, la tariffa**
farm **la fattoria**
farmer **l'agricoltore** (m)
fashion **la moda**
fast **veloce**
fat **il grasso;** (adj) **grasso**
father **il padre**
February **febbraio**
feel (touch) **tastare;** *I feel hot* **ho caldo;** *I feel like ...* **ho voglia di ...;** *I don't feel well* **non mi sento bene**
fence **lo steccato**
fennel **il finocchio**
ferry **il traghetto**
fever **la febbre**
fiancé **il fidanzato**
fiancée **la fidanzata**
field **il campo**
fifteen **quindici**
fifty **cinquanta**
figures **le cifre**
filling (in tooth) **l'otturazione** (f); (in sandwich, cake, etc.) **il ripieno**
film (for camera) **la pellicola;** (at the movies) **il film**
filter **il filtro**
financial consultant **il/la consulente finanziario**
fine! **benissimo!**
finger **il dito**
fire **il fuoco;** (blaze) **l'incendio** (m)
fire extinguisher **l'estintore** (m)
fireplace **il caminetto**
fireworks **i fuochi d'artificio**
first **primo;** *first class* **prima classe**
first aid **il pronto soccorso**
first name **il nome di battesimo**
fish **il pesce**
fishing **la pesca;** *to go fishing* **andare a pesca**
fishmonger (shop) **la pescheria**
five **cinque**
fizzy **frizzante**
flag **la bandiera**
flash (camera) **il flash**
flat (level) **piatto;** (apartment) **l'appartamento**
flavor **il gusto**
flashlight **la torcia** (elettrica)
flea **la pulce**
flight **il volo;** *flight number* **il numero del volo**
flipflops **gli infradito**
flippers **le pinne**
floor (ground) **il pavimento;** (story) **il piano**
Florence **Firenze**
flour **la farina**
flower **il fiore;** *flower bed* **l'aiuola** (f)
flute **il flauto**
fly (insect) **la mosca;** (verb) **volare;** *I'm flying to London* **vado a Londra in aereo**
flysheet **il telo protettivo**
fog **la nebbia**
folk music **la musica folk**
food **il cibo**
food poisoning **l'intossicazione alimentare** (f)
foot **il piede;** *on foot* **a piedi**
for **per;** *for me* **per me;** *what for?* **perché?**
forbidden **proibito**
foreigner **lo straniero, il forestiero**
forest **la foresta**
forget **dimenticare**
fork (for food) **la forchetta**
forty **quaranta**
four **quattro**
fourteen **quattordici**
fourth **quarto**
fracture **la frattura**
France **la Francia**
free (not occupied) **libero;** (no charge) **gratuito, gratis**
freezer **il congelatore**
French **francese**
french fries **le patatine fritte**
Friday **venerdì**
fried **fritto**
friend **l'amico;** (female) **l'amica**
friendly **cordiale**
frightened: *I'm frightened* **ho paura**
front: *in front of you* **davanti a te**
frost **il gelo**
frozen foods **i surgelati**
fruit **la frutta**
fruit juice **il succo di frutta**
fry **friggere**
frying pan **la padella**
full **pieno;** *I'm full* **sono sazio**

full board **la pensione completa**
funny **divertente;** (odd) **strano**
furniture **i mobili**

G

garage **il garage**
garbage **le immondizie, la spazzatura**
garbage bag **il sacchetto per la pattumiera**
garbage can **la pattumiera**
garden **il giardino;** *garden center* **il vivaio**
gardener **il giardiniere**
garlic **l'aglio** (m)
gasoline **la benzina**
gas-permeable lenses **le lenti semi-rigide**
gas station **il benzinaio, la stazione di servizio**
gate **il cancello;** (at airport) **l'uscita** (f)
gay (homosexual) **omosessuale, gay**
gearbox (car) **il cambio**
gear stick **la leva del cambio**
gel (hair) **il gel**
Genoa **Genova**
German **tedesco**
Germany **la Germania**
get (obtain) **ricevere;** (fetch: person) **chiamare;** (something) **prendere;** *do you have ...?* **ha ...?;** *to get the train* **prendere il treno**
get back: we get back tomorrow **torniamo domani;** *to get something back* **riavere indietro qualcosa**
get in **entrare;** (arrive) **arrivare**
get off (bus, etc.) **scendere (da)**
get on (bus, etc.) **salire (su)**
get out **uscire (da)**
get up **alzarsi**
gift **il regalo**
gin **il gin**
ginger (spice) **lo zenzero**
girl **la ragazza**
give **dare;**
glad **contento**
glass (material) **il vetro;** (for drinking) **il bicchiere**
glasses **gli occhiali**
gloves **i guanti**
glue **la colla**
go **andare;** (depart) **partire**
gold **l'oro** (m)

golf **il golf**
golfer **il golfista**
good **buono;** *good!* **bene!**
goodbye **arrivederci**
good day **buongiorno**
good evening **buonasera**
good night **buonanotte**
government **il governo**
granddaughter **la nipote**
grandfather **il nonno**
grandmother **la nonna**
grandparents **i nonni**
grandson **il nipote**
grapes **l'uva** (f)
grass **l'erba** (f)
gray **grigio**
great! **benissimo!**
Great Britain **la Gran Bretagna**
Greece **la Grecia**
Greek **greco**
green **verde**
grill **la griglia**
grilled **alla griglia**
grocery store **gli alimentari**
ground floor **il pianterreno**
groundsheet **il telone impermeabile**
guarantee **la garanzia;** (verb) **garantire**
guard **la guardia**
guest **l'ospite** (m/f)
guide (person) **la guida**
guidebook **la guida**
guitar **la chitarra**
gun (rifle) **il fucile;** (pistol) **la pistola**
gutter **la grondaia**
guy rope **la corda**
gymnastics **la palestra**

H

hair **i capelli**
haircut **il taglio**
hairdresser **il parrucchiere**
hair dryer **il fohn**
hairspray **la lacca per i capelli**
half **metà;** *half an hour* **mezz'ora;** *half board* **mezza pensione;** *half past ... ... e mezza*
ham **il prosciutto**
hamburger **l'hamburger** (m)
hammer **il martello**
hamster **il criceto**
hand brake **il freno a mano**
hand **la mano;** *hand luggage* **il bagaglio a mano**
handle (door) **la maniglia**
handshake **la stretta di mano**

handsome **bello, attraente**
handyman **il muratore**
hangover **i postumi della sbornia**
happy **felice, contento**
harbor **il porto**
hard **duro;** (difficult) **difficile**
hardware store **la ferramenta**
hat **il cappello**
have **avere;** *I don't have ...* **non ho ...;** *do you have ...?* **ha ...?;** *I have to go now* **devo andare adesso**
he **lui**
head **la testa**
headache **il mal di testa**
headlights **i fari**
headquarters **la sede centrale**
hear **udire, sentire**
hearing aid **l'apparecchio acustico** (m)
heart **il cuore**
heart condition **il disturbi cardiaci**
hearts (cards) **i cuori**
heater **il termosifone**
heating **il riscaldamento**
heavy **pesante**
hedge **la siepe**
heel (of foot) **il tallone;** (of shoe) **il tacco**
hello **ciao, buongiorno;** (on phone) **pronto**
help **l'aiuto** (m); (verb) **aiutare;** *can I help you?* **dica?**
her **lei, suo, sua, sue, suoi;** *it's for her* **è per lei;** *her book* **il suo libro;** *her house* **la sua casa;** *her shoes* **le sue scarpe;** *her dresses* **i suoi vestiti;** *it's hers* **è suo**
herbal tea **la tisana**
here **qui**
here you are/here it is **ecco**
hi! **Ciao!**
high **alto**
hiking **l'escursionismo**
hill **la collina**
him: it's for him **è per lui;** *give it to him* **daglielo**
his **suo, sua, sue, suoi;** *his book* **il suo libro;** *his house* **la sua casa;** *his shoes* **le sue scarpe;** *his socks* **i suoi calzini;** *it's his* **è suo**
history **la storia**
hitchhike **fare l'autostop**
HIV-positive **HIV positivo**
hobby **il passatempo, il hobby**

holiday **il giorno festivo**
home: at home **a casa**
homeopathy **omeopatia**
honest **onesto**
honey **il miele**
honeymoon **la luna di miele**
hood (car) **il cofano**
horn (car) **il clacson**; (animal) **il corno**
horrible **orribile**
hose **il tubo**
hospital **l'ospedale** (m)
host **il padrone di casa**; hostess **la padrona di casa**
hot **caldo**
hour **l'ora** (f); visiting hours **l'orario di visita** (f)
house **la casa**
household products **gli articoli per la casa**
how? **come?**
how much? **quanto costa?**; how much is that? **quant'è?**
hundred **cento**; three hundred **trecento**
hungry: I'm hungry **ho fame**
hurry **affrettarsi**; I'm in a hurry **ho fretta**
hurry up! **sbrigati!**
hurt: my ... hurts **mi fa male il/ la ...**; will it hurt? **farà male?**
husband **il marito**

I
I **io**
ice **il ghiaccio**
ice cream **il gelato**
ice skates **i pattini da ghiaccio**
identification **il documento d'identità**
if **se**
ignition **l'accensione** (f)
ill **malato**
immediately **immediatamente**
impossible **impossibile**
in: in English **in inglese**; in the hotel **nell'albergo**; in Venice **a Venezia**
included **incluso**
indigestion **l'indigestione** (f)
infection **l'infezione** (f)
information **le informazioni**; information technology **l'informatica** (f)
inhaler (for asthma, etc.) **l'inalatore** (m)
injection **l'iniezione** (m)
injury **la ferita**
ink **l'inchiostro** (m)
in-laws **i suoceri**

inner tube **la camera d'aria**
insect **l'insetto** (m)
insect repellent **l'insettifugo** (m)
insomnia **l'insonnia** (f)
instant coffee **il caffè solubile**
insurance **l'assicurazione** (f)
interesting **interessante**
Internet **l'internet** (f)
interpret **interpretare**
interpreter **l'interprete** (m/f)
intersection **l'incrocio** (m)
intravenous drip **la flebo**
invitation **l'invito** (m)
invoice **la fattura**
Ireland **l'Irlanda** (f)
Irish **irlandese**
iron (material) **il ferro**; (for clothes) **il ferro da stiro**; (verb) **stirare**
is: he/she/it is ... **(lui/lei/esso) è ...**
island **l'isola** (f)
it **esso**
Italian **italiano**
Italy **Italia**
its **suo**

J
jacket **la giacca**
jam **la marmellata**
January **gennaio**
jazz **il jazz**
jeans **i jeans**
jellyfish **la medusa**
jeweler (shop) **il gioielliere**
job **il lavoro**
jog (verb) **fare jogging**; to go jogging **andare a fare jogging**
jogging **il jogging**
jogging suit **la tuta da ginnastica**
joke **lo scherzo**
journey **il viaggio**
July **luglio**
June **giugno**
just (only) **solo**; it's just arrived **è appena arrivato**

K
kerosene **la paraffina**
key **la chiave**
keyboard **la tastiera**
kidney **il rene**
kilo **il chilo**
kilometer **il chilometro**
kitchen **la cucina**
knee **il ginocchio**
knife **il coltello**

knit **lavorare a maglia**
knitwear **la maglieria**
know **sapere**; (person) **conoscere**; I don't know **non so**

L
label **l'etichetta** (f)
lace **il pizzo**
laces (of shoe) **i lacci**
lady **la signora**
lake **il lago**
lamb **l'agnello** (m)
lamp **la lampada**
lampshade **il paralume**
land **la terra**; (verb) **atterrare**
language **la lingua**
laptop (computer) **il computer portatile**
large **grande**
last (final) **ultimo**; last week **la settimana scorsa**; at last! **finalmente!**
last name **il cognome**
late: it's getting late **si sta facendo tardi**; the bus is late **l'autobus è in ritardo**
later **più tardi**
laugh **ridere**
laundry (place) **la lavanderia**; (dirty clothes) **la biancheria**
laundry detergent **il detersivo** (per bucato)
law **la legge**
lawn **il prato**; lawnmower **il tosaerba**
lawyer **l'avvocato**
laxative **il lassativo**
lazy **pigro**
leaf **la foglia**
leaflet **il volantino**
learn **imparare**
leash (for dog) **il guinzaglio**
leather **la pelle, il cuoio**; leather goods shop **la pelletteria**
lecture hall **l'aula delle lezioni** (f)
left (not right) **sinistra**; there's nothing left **non c'è rimasto più nulla**
left luggage locker **il desposito bagagli**
leg **la gamba**
lemon **il limone**
lemonade **la limonata**
length **la lunghezza**
lens **la lente**
less **meno**

lesson **la lezione**
letter **la lettera**
lettuce **la lattuga**
library **la biblioteca**
license **la patente**
license plate **la targa**
life **la vita**
light **la luce;** *(not heavy)* **leggero;** *(not dark)* **chiaro**
light bulb **la lampadina**
lighter **l'accendino** (m)
lighter fuel **il gas per accendini**
light meter **l'esposimetro** (m)
like: I like ... **mi piace ...;** *it's like ...* **assomiglia a ...;** *like this one* **come questo**
lime (fruit) **il limoncello**
line (telephone, etc.) **la linea;** *outside line* **la linea esterna**
line (waiting) **la fila;** *stand in line* **fare la fila**
lipstick **il rossetto**
liqueur **il liquore**
list **l'elenco** (m)
liter **il litro**
literature **la letteratura**
litter (bin) **i rifiuti**
little (small) **piccolo;** *it's a little big* **è un po' grande;** *just a little* **solo un po'**
liver **il fegato**
living room **il soggiorno**
lollipop **il lecca lecca**
long **lungo;** *how long does it take?* **quanto ci vuole?**
long-distance (call) **interurbana**
lost: I'm lost **mi sono persa**
lost property **l'ufficio oggetti smarriti** (m)
lot: a lot **molto**
loud **forte**
love (verb) **amare**
low **basso**
luck **la fortuna;** *good luck!* **buona fortuna!**
luggage **i bagagli**
luggage rack **la reticella (per i bagagli)**
lunch **il pranzo**

M

madam **signora**
magazine **la rivista**
maid **la cameriera**
mail **la posta;** (verb) **spedire per posta**

mailbox **la cassetta delle lettere**
mail carrier **il postino**
main courses **i secondi piatti**
make **fare**
makeup **il trucco**
man **l'uomo;** *men* **gli uomini**
manager **il direttore/ la direttrice**
many **molti;** *not many* **non molti**
map **la carta** (geografica); (of town) **la pianta**
marble **il marmo**
March **marzo**
margarine **la margarina**
market **il mercato**
marmalade **la marmellata d'arance**
married **sposato**
mascara **il mascara**
mass (church) **la messa**
mast **l'albero** (m)
match (light) **il fiammifero;** (sports) **l'incontro** (m)
material (cloth) **la stoffa**
matter: it doesn't matter **non importa;** *what's the matter* **cosa c'è?**
mattress **il materasso**
May **maggio**
maybe **forse**
me: it's me **sono io;** *it's for me* **è per me**
meal **il pasto**
mean: what does this mean? **che cosa significa?**
meat **la carne**
mechanic **il meccanico**
medicine **la medicina**
Mediterranean **il Mediterraneo**
meeting **la riunione, l'incontro** (m)
melon **il melone**
menu **il menù**
message **il messaggio**
microwave **il forno a microonde**
middle: in the middle of the square **in mezzo alla piazza;** *in the middle of the night* **nel cuore della notte**
midnight **mezzanotte**
Milan **Milano**
milk **il latte**
million **milione**
mine: it's mine **è mio**

mineral water **l'acqua minerale** (f)
minute **il minuto**
mirror **lo specchio**
Miss **Signorina**
mistake **l'errore** (m)
modem **il modem**
mom **mamma**
Monday **lunedì**
money **i soldi**
monitor (computer) **il monitor**
month **il mese**
monument **il monumento**
moon **la luna**
moped **il motorino**
more **più;** *more than ...* **più di ...**
morning **la mattina;** *in the morning* **di mattina**
mosaic **il mosaico**
mosquito **la zanzara**
mother **la madre**
motorboat **il motoscafo**
motorcycle **la motocicletta**
mountain **la montagna**
mountain bike **il mountain bike**
mouse (animal) **il topo;** (computer) **il mouse**
mousse (for hair) **la schiuma**
mouth **la bocca**
move **muovere;** *don't move!* **non muoverti!**
move house **traslocare**
movie theater **il cinema**
Mr. **Signor**
Mrs. **Signora**
much **molto;** *much better* **molto meglio;** *much slower* **molto più lentamente;** *not much* **non molto**
mug **il tazzone**
museum **il museo**
mushroom **il fungo**
music **la musica**
musical instrument **lo strumento musicale**
musician **il musicista**
music system **lo stereo**
mussels **le cozze**
must (to have to) **devore;** *I must* **devo**
mustache **i baffi**
mustard **la senape**
my **mio, mia, mie, miei;** *my book* **il mio libro;** *my bag* **la mia borsa;** *my keys* **le mie chiavi;** *my dresses* **i miei vestiti**

N

nail (metal) **il chiodo**; (finger)
  l'unghia (f)
nail clippers **il tagliaunghie**
nail file **la limetta per le
  unghie**
nail polish **lo smalto per le
  unghie**
name **il nome**; *what's your
  name?* **come si chiama/ti
  chiami?** (formal/informal);
  my name's ... **mi chiamo...**
napkin **il tovagliolo**
Naples **Napoli**
narrow **stretto**
near **vicino**; *near to ...* **vicino a ...**
necessary **necessario,
  obbligatorio**
neck **il collo**
necklace **la collana**
need **avere bisogno**; *I need ...*
  ho bisogno di ...; *there's
  no need* **non c'è bisogno**
needle **l'ago** (m)
negative (photo) **la negativa**;
  (adj) **negativo**
nephew **il nipote**
never **mai**
new **nuovo**
news **le notizie**; (on radio)
  il notiziario
newsstand **il giornalaio**
newspaper **il giornale**
New Zealand **la Nuova Zelanda**
New Zealander **neozelandese**
next **prossimo**; *next week* **la
  settimana prossima**;
  what next? **e poi?**; *who's
  next?* **a chi tocca?**
nice (attractive) **carino, bello**;
  (pleasant) **simpatico**;
  (to eat) **buono**
niece **la nipote**
night **la notte**
nightclub **il night**
nightgown **la camicia da notte**
nightstand **il comodino**
nine **nove**
nineteen **diciannove**
ninety **novanta**
no (negative response) **no**; *I
  have no money* **non ho soldi**
nobody **nessuno**
no entry **divieto di accesso**
noisy **rumoroso**
noon **il mezzogiorno**
north **il nord**
Northern Ireland **l'Irlanda
  del Nord**
nose **il naso**

not **non**; *he's not ...* **non è ...**
notebook **il quaderno**
notepad **il bloc-notes**
nothing **niente**
novel **il romanzo**
November **novembre**
now **ora, adesso**
nowhere **da nessuna parte**
number **il numero**
nurse **il infermiere/la
  infermiera**
nut **la noce, la nocciola**; (for
  bolt) **il dado**

O

oars **i remi**
occasionally **ogni tanto**
occupied **occupato**
o'clock: one o'clock **l'una**; *two
  o'clock* **le due**
occupied (restroom) **occupato**
October **ottobre**
octopus **la piovra, il polipo**
of **di**
office **l'ufficio** (m), **la
  direzione**; *office worker*
  l'impiegato/a
often **spesso**
oil **l'olio** (m)
ointment **la pomata,
  l'unguento** (m)
OK **OK**
old **vecchio**; *how old are you?*
  quanti anni hai?
olive **l'oliva** (f)
olive oil **l'olio d'oliva** (m)
omelet **l'omelette** (f)
on **su**; *a book on Venice* **un
  libro su Venezia**; *on
  Monday* **di lunedì**
one **uno**
one way **senso unico**
one-way ticket **il biglietto di
  sola andata**
onion **la cipolla**
only **solo**
open (adj) **aperto**; (verb) **aprire**
opera **l'opera** (f)
operating room **la sala
  operatoria**
operation **l'operazione** (f)
operator **l'operatore/
  l'operatrice** (m/f)
opposite **davanti a**
optician **l'ottico** (m)
or **o**
orange (fruit) **l'arancia** (f);
  (color) **arancione**
orange juice **il succo
  d'arancia**

orchestra **l'orchestra** (f);
  (theater seating) **la platea**
order (for goods) **l'ordinativo**
  (m), **l'ordine** (m)
ordinary **normale**
organ (music) **l'organo** (m)
other: the other (one) **l'altro**
our: our hotel **il nostro
  albergo**; *our car* **la nostra
  macchina**; *it's ours* **è nostro**
out: he's out **è uscito**
outside **fuori**
oven **il forno**
over (above) **su, sopra**; *over
  100* **più di cento**; *over the
  river* **al di là del fiume**; *it's
  over* (finished) **è finito**; *over
  there* **laggiù**
overpass **il cavalcavia**

P

pacifier (for baby) **il ciuccio**
package, packet **il pacchetto**
padlock **il lucchetto**
Padua **Padova**
page **la pagina**
pain **il dolore**
paint **la vernice**
painting **la pittura**
pair **il paio**
pajamas **il pigiama**
palace **il palazzo**
pale **pallido**
paper **la carta**; (newspaper)
  il giornale
pants **i pantaloni**
pantyhose (sheer) **i collant**
parcel **il pacco**
pardon? **prego?**
parents **i genitori**
park **il parco**; (verb)
  parcheggiare; *no parking*
  sosta vietata
parking lights **le luci di
  posizione**
parking lot **il parcheggio**
parsley **il prezzemolo**
part (hair) **la riga**
party (celebration) **la festa**;
  (group) **il gruppo**;
  (political) **il partito**
pass (driving) **sorpassare**
passenger **il passeggero**;
  (female) **la passeggera**
passport **il passaporto**;
  passport control **il controllo
  passaporti**
password **la password**
pasta **la pasta**
path **il vialetto, il sentiero**

pay **pagare**
payment **il pagamento**
peach **la pesca**
peanuts **le arachidi**
pear **la pera**
pearl **la perla**
peas **i piselli**
pedestrian **il pedone**
pedestrian zone **la zona pedonale**
peg (tent) **il picchetto**
pen **la penna**
pencil **la matita**
pencil sharpener **il temperamatite**
penicillin **la penicillina**
penknife **il temperino**
pen pal **il/la corrispondente**
people **la gente**
pepper (spice)**il pepe;** (vegetable) **il peperone**
peppermint **la menta piperita**
per: per person **a persona;** per annum **all'anno**
perfect **perfetto**
perfume **il profumo**
perhaps **magari, forse**
perm **la permanente**
pharmacy **la farmacia**
phone card **la scheda telefonica**
photocopier **la fotocopiatrice**
photograph **la fotografia;** (verb) **fotografare**
photographer **il fotografo**
phrasebook **il vocabolarietto**
pickpocket **il borsaiolo**
pickup (postal) **la levata**
picnic **il picnic**
piece **il pezzo**
pillow **il guanciale**
PIN **il pin, il codice segreto**
pin **lo spillo**
pineapple **l'ananas (m)**
pink **rosa**
pipe (for smoking) **la pipa;** (for water) **il tubo**
piston **il pistone**
place **il posto;** at your place **a casa tua**
planner **l'agenda (f)**
plans **le piante**
plant **la pianta**
plastic **la plastica**
plastic bag **il sacchetto di plastica**
plate **il piatto**
platform **il binario**
play (theater) **la commedia;** (verb) **giocare**

please **per favore**
pleased to meet you **piacere**
plug (electrical) **la spina;** (sink) **il tappo**
plumber **il idraulico**
pocket **la tasca**
poison **il veleno**
police **la polizia**
police officer **il poliziotto**
police report **il rapporto di polizia**
police station **la stazione di polizia**
politics **la politica**
poor **povero**
poor quality **di cattiva qualità**
pop music **la musica pop**
Pope **il Papa**
pork **la carne di maiale**
port **il porto**
porter (hotel) **il portiere**
possible **possibile**
postcard **la cartolina**
post office **l'ufficio postale (m)**
potato **la patata**
poultry **il pollame**
pound (weight) **la libbra;** (currency) **la sterlina**
prefer **preferire**
pregnant **incinta**
prescription **la ricetta**
presentation **la conferenza**
pretty (beautiful) **grazioso, carino;** (quite) **piuttosto**
price **il prezzo**
priest **il prete**
printer **la stampante**
private **privato**
problem **il problema;** no problem **non c'è problema**
profits **i profitti**
public **pubblico**
pull **tirare**
puncture **la foratura**
purple **viola**
purse **il borsellino**
push **spingere**
pushchair **il passegino**
put **mettere**

Q
quality **la qualità**
quarter **il quarto;** quarter past ... ... **e un quarto**
question **la domanda**
quick **veloce**
quiet **tranquillo**
quite (fairly) **abbastanza;** (fully) **molto**

R
rabbit **il coniglio (m)**
radiator **il radiatore**
radio **la radio**
radish **il ravanello**
railroad **la ferrovia**
rain **la pioggia**
raincoat **l'impermeabile (m)**
raisins **l'uvetta (f)**
rake **il rastrello**
rare (uncommon) **raro;** (meat) **al sangue**
rash **il arrossamento**
raspberry **il lampone**
rat **il ratto**
razor blades **le lamette**
read **leggere**
reading lamp **la lampada da studio**
ready **pronto**
realtor **l'agente immobiliare (m/f)**
rear lights **i fari posteriori**
receipt (restaurants, hotels) **la ricevuta;** (shops, bars) **lo scontrino**
reception (party) **il rinfresco;** (hotel) **la reception**
receptionist **il/la receptionist**
record (music) **il disco;** (sports, etc.) **il record**
record store **il negozio di dischi**
red **rosso**
refreshments **i rinfreschi**
refrigerator **il frigorifero**
registered (mail) **raccomandata**
relax **rilassarsi**
relief: what a relief! **che sollievo!**
religion **la religione**
remember **ricordare;** I don't remember **non ricordo**
rent (verb) **affittare, noleggiare**
repair **riparare**
report **la relazione**
research **la ricerca**
reservation **la prenotazione**
rest (noun: remainder) **il resto;** (verb: to relax) **riposarsi**
restaurant **il ristorante**
return **ritornare;** (give back) **restituire**
rice **il riso**
rich **ricco**
right (correct) **giusto, esatto;** (not left) **destro**

ring (jewelry) **l'anello** (m)
ripe **maturo**
river **il fiume**
road **la strada**
roasted **arrosto**
rock (stone) **la roccia**; (music) **il rock**
roll (bread) **il panino**
Rome **Roma**
roof **il tetto**
room **la stanza, la camera**; (space) **lo spazio**; room service **il servizio in camera**
rope **la corda**
rose **la rosa**
round (circular) **rotondo**
roundabout **la rotatoria**
round-trip ticket **il biglietto di andata e ritorno**
row **remare**
rubber band **l'elastico** (m)
ruby (gem) **il rubino**
rug (mat) **il tappeto**
rugby **il rugby**
ruins **le rovine, i resti**
ruler (for drawing) **la riga**
rum **il rum**
run (verb) **correre**

S

sad **triste**
safe (not dangerous) **sicuro**
safety pin **la spilla di sicurezza**
sailing **la vela**
salad **l'insalata** (f)
salami **il salame**
sale (at reduced prices) **i saldi**
sales (of goods, etc.) **le vendite**
salmon **il salmone**
salt **il sale**
same: the same dress **lo stesso vestito**; same again, please **un altro, per favore**
sand **la sabbia**
sandals **i sandali**
sand dunes **le dune**
sandwich **il panino**
sanitary napkins **gli assorbenti** (igienici)
Sardinia **la Sardegna**
Saturday **sabato**
sauce **la salsa**
saucepan **la pentola**
saucer **il piattino**
sauna **la sauna**
sausage **la salsiccia**

say **dire**; what did you say? **che cosa ha detto?**; how do you say ...? **come si dice ...?**
scarf **la sciarpa**; (head) **il foulard**
schedule **l'orario** (m)
school **la scuola**
science **la scienza**
scissors **le forbici**
Scotland **la Scozia**
Scotsman **lo scozzese**
Scotswoman **la scozzese**
Scottish **scozzese**
screen **lo schermo**
screw **la vite**
screwdriver **il cacciavite**
sea **il mare**
seafood **i frutti di mare**
seat **il posto**
seat belt **la cintura di sicurezza**
second **secondo**; second class **seconda classe**; second floor **il primo piano**
secretary **il segretario/la segretaria**
see **vedere**; I can't see **non vedo**; I see (understand) **capisco, vedo**
self-employed **libero professionista**
sell **vendere**
seminar **il seminario**
send **mandare**
separate (adj) **separato**
separated (couple) **separati**
September **settembre**
serious **serio**; (illness) **grave**
seven **sette**
seventeen **diciassette**
seventy **settanta**
several **diversi**
sew **cucire**
shampoo **lo shampoo**
shave (verb) **radersi**
shaving cream **la schiuma \da barba**
shawl **lo scialle**
she **lei**
sheers **le cesoie**
sheet **il lenzuolo**
shell **la conchiglia**
shellfish (crabs, etc.) **i crostacei**; (mollusks) **i molluschi**
sherry **lo sherry**
ship **la nave**
shirt **la camicia**
shoelaces **i lacci per le scarpe**

shoe polish **il lucido per le scarpe**
shoe repairer **il calzolaio**
shoes **le scarpe**
shop **il negozio**
shopkeeper **il/la commerciante**
shopping **lo shopping, la spesa**; to go shopping **andare a fare acquisti**; (for food) **andare a fare la spesa**
short **basso, corto**
shorts **gli short**
shoulder **la spalla**
shower **la doccia**; (rain) **l'acquazzone** (m)
shower gel **la docciaschiuma** (f)
shutter (camera) **l'otturatore** (m); (window) **l'imposta** (f), **le persiane**
Sicily **la Sicilia**
side (edge) **il lato**
sidewalk **il marciapiede**
sign (in station, etc.) **il cartello**; (road, etc.) **l'insegna** (f)
sign (verb) **firmare**
silk **la seta**
silver (color) **d'argento**; (metal) **l'argento** (m)
simple **semplice**
sing **cantare**
single (one) **solo**; (unmarried: man) **celibe**; (woman) **nubile**
single room **la camera singola**
sink **il lavabo, il lavandino**; (kitchen) **il lavello**
sir **signore**
sister **la sorella**
site (in campground, etc.) **la piazzola**
six **sei**
sixteen **sedici**
sixty **sessanta**
size (clothes) **la taglia**; (shoe) **il numero**
skid **slittare**
skiing: to go skiing **andare a sciare**
skin cleanser **il latte detergente**
ski resort **la località sciistica**
skirt **la gonna**
skis **gli sci**
sky **il cielo**
sleep **il sonno**; (verb) **dormire**
sleeper car **il vagone letto**
sleeping bag **il sacco a pelo**
sleeping pill **il sonnifero**
sleeve **la manica**
slippers **le pantofole**

slow **lento**
small **piccolo**
smell **l'odore** (m); (verb: to stink) **puzzare**
smile **il sorriso**; (verb) **sorridere**
smoke **il fumo**; (verb) **fumare**
smoking (section) **fumatori**; nonsmoking **non fumatori**
snack **lo spuntino**
snorkel **il boccaglio**
snow **la neve**
so **così**; so good **così bene**; not so much **non così tanto**
soaking solution (for contact lenses) **il liquido per lenti**
soap **il sapone**
soccer (game) **il calcio**; (ball) **il pallone**
socks **i calzini**
soda water **l'acqua di seltz** (f)
sofa **il divano**
soft **morbido**
soil **la terra**
somebody **qualcuno**
somehow in **qualche modo**
something **qualcosa**
sometimes **qualche volta**
somewhere **da qualche parte**
son **il figlio**
song **la canzone**
sorry! **scusi!**; I'm sorry **mi dispiace, spiacente**; sorry? (pardon) **come?, scusi?**
soup **la minestra, la zuppa**
south **il sud**
souvenir **il souvenir**
spade (shovel) **la vanga**
spades (cards) **le picche**
Spain **la Spagna**
Spanish **spagnolo**
spare parts (car) **i pezzi di ricambio**
spark plug **la candela**
sparkling water **l'acqua gassata** (f)
speak **parlare**; do you speak ...? **parla ...?**; I don't speak ... **non parlo ...**
speed **la velocità**
SPF (sun protection factor) **il fattore di protezione**
spider **il ragno**
spinach **gli spinaci**
spoon **il cucchiaio**
sports **lo sport**
spring (mechanical) **la molla**; (season) **la primavera**
square (noun: in town) **la piazza**; (adj: shape) **quadrato**

staircase **la scala**
stairs **le scale**
stamp **il francobollo**
stapler **la cucitrice, la spillatrice**
star **la stella**; (film) **la star**
start **l'inizio** (m); (verb) **cominciare**
statement (to police) **la denuncia**
station **la stazione**
statue **la statua**
steal **rubare**; it's been stolen **è stato rubato**
steamed **a vapore**
steamer (boat) **la nave a vapore**; (for cooking) **la pentola a pressione**
still water **l'acqua naturale** (f)
stockings **le calze**
stomach **lo stomaco**
stomachache **il mal di pancia**
stop (noun: bus) **la fermata dell'autobus**; (verb) **fermare**; stop! **alt!, fermo!**
storm **la tempesta**
stove **il cucina**
stove fuel **il gas da campeggio**
straight ahead **sempre dritto**
strawberry **la fragola**
stream **il ruscello**
street **la strada**
string (cord) **lo spago**; (guitar, etc.) **la corda**
strong **forte**
student **lo studente/la studentessa** (m/f)
stuffy **soffocante**
stupid **stupido**
suburbs **la periferia**
subway **la metro** (politana)
sugar **lo zucchero**
suit **il completo**; it suits you **ti sta bene**
suitcase **la valigia**
summer **l'estate** (f)
sun **il sole**
sunbathe **prendere il sole**
sunburn **l'eritema solare** (m)
Sunday **domenica**
sunglasses **gli occhiali da sole**
sunny: it's sunny **c'è il sole**
sunshade **l'ombrellone** (m)
suntan: to get **a suntan abbronzarsi**
suntan lotion **la lozione solare**
suntanned **abbronzato**
supermarket **il supermercato**
supper **la cena**

supplement **il supplemento**
suppository **la supposta**
sure **sicuro**; are you sure? **sei sicuro?**
sweat **il sudore**; (verb) **sudare**
sweater **il maglione**
sweatshirt **la felpa**
sweet **la caramella**; (not sour) **dolce**
swim (verb) **nuotare**
swimming **il nuoto**
swimming pool **la piscina**
swimming trunks **il costume da bagno** (per uomo)
swimsuit **il costume da bagno**
Swiss **lo svizzerola/la svizzera**; (adj) **svizzero**
switch **l'interruttore** (m)
Switzerland **la Svizzera**
synagogue **la sinagoga**
syrup **lo sciroppo**

T

table **il tavolo**
tablet **la compressa**
take **prendere**
takeoff **il decollo**
talcum powder **il talco**
talk **la conversazione**; (verb) **parlare**
tall **alto**
tampons **i tamponi**
tangerine **il mandarino**
tap **il rubinetto**
tapestry **l'arazzo** (m)
taxi **il taxi**
taxi stand **il posteggio dei taxi**
tea **il tè**; tea with milk **il tè con latte**
teach **insegnare**
teacher **l'insegnante**
teakettle **il bollitore**
technician **il tecnico**
telephone **il telefono**; (verb) **telefonare**
telephone booth **la cabina telefonica**
telephone call **la telefonata**
telephone number **il numero di telefono**
television **la televisione**
temperature **la temperatura**; (fever) **la febbre**
ten **dieci**
tennis **il tennis**
tent **la tenda**
tent pole **il palo della tenda**
terminal (airport) **il terminale**

terrace **il patio**
test **il controllo**
than **di**
thank (verb) **ringraziare;**
   thank you/thanks **grazie**
that: that one **quello;** *that*
   country **quel paese;** *that*
   man **quell'uomo;** *that*
   woman **quella donna;**
   what's that? **cos'è quello?;**
   I think that ... **penso che**
   ...; *that'll be all* **basta così**
the **il/lo** (m); **la** (f); **i/gli** (m pl);
   le (f pl)
theater **il teatro**
their: their room **la loro**
   stanza; *their friend* **il loro**
   amico; *their books* **i loro**
   libri; *their pens* **le loro**
   penne; *it's theirs* **è loro**
them: it's for them **è per loro;**
   give it to them **dallo a loro**
then **poi, allora**
there **là;** *there is/are ...* **c'è/ci**
   sono ...; *is/are there ...?* **c'è/**
   ci sono ...?
these: these things **queste cose;**
   these boys **questi ragazzi**
they **loro**
thick **spesso**
thief **il ladro**
thin **magro**
think **pensare;** *I think so*
   penso di sì; *I'll think about*
   it **ci penserò**
third **terzo**
thirsty: I'm thirsty **ho sete**
thirteen **tredici**
thirty **trenta**
this: this one **questo;** *this*
   picture **questo quadro;**
   this man **quest'uomo;** *this*
   woman **questa donna;**
   what's this? **cos'è questo?;**
   this is Mr ... **(questo è)**
   il signor ...
those: those things **quelle**
   cose; *those boys*
   quei ragazzi
thousand **mille**
three **tre**
throat **la gola**
throat lozenges **le**
   pasticche per la gola
through **attraverso**
thumbtack **la puntina da**
   disegno
thunderstorm **il temporale**
Thursday **giovedì**
Tiber **il Tevere**
ticket **il biglietto**

ticket office **la biglietteria**
tide **la marea**
tie **la cravatta;** (verb) **legare**
tight (clothes) **stretto**
tights (wool) **la calzamaglia**
tile **la piastrella**
time **il tempo;** *what's time is it?*
   che ore sono?; *opening times*
   l'orario di apertura (m);
   leisure time **il tempo libero**
tin **la scatola**
tip (money) **la mancia;** (end)
   la punta
tire **la gomma;** *flat tire*
   la gomma a
   terratirato stanco
tissues **i fazzolettini di carta**
to: to England in **Inghilterra;**
   to the station **alla stazione;**
   to the doctor **dal dottore;**
   to the center **in centro**
toast **il pane tostato**
tobacco **il tabacco**
tobacconist (shop) **il**
   tabaccaio
today **oggi**
together **insieme**
toilet **la toilette**
toilet paper **la carta igienica**
tomato **il pomodoro**
tomato juice **il succo**
   di pomodoro
tomorrow **domani;** *see you*
   tomorrow **a domani**
tongue **la lingua**
tonic **l'acqua tonica** (f)
tonight **stasera**
too (also) **anche;** (excessively)
   troppo
tooth **il dente**
toothache **il mal di denti**
toothbrush **lo spazzolino**
   da denti
toothpaste **il dentifricio**
tour **il giro;** *guided tour* **la**
   visita guidata
tourist **il/la turista**
tourist information **l'azienda**
   turistica (f); (office)
   l'ufficio turistico (m)
towel **l'asciugamano** (m)
tower **la torre;** *Leaning Tower*
   of Pisa **la Torre di Pisa**
town **la città**
town hall **il municipio**
toy **il giocattolo**
toy store **il negozio di**
   giocattoli
tractor **il trattore**
tradition **la tradizione**
traffic **il traffico**

traffic jam **l'ingorgo** (m)
traffic lights **il semaforo**
trailer **il rimorchio, la**
   roulotte
train **il treno**
translate **tradurre**
translator **il traduttore/la**
   traduttrice
travel **viaggiare**
travel agent **l'agenzia**
   di viaggio (f)
tray **il vassoio**
tree **l'albero** (m)
truck **il camion**
trunk (of car) **il bagagliaio**
true **vero**
try **provare**
Tuesday **martedì**
tunnel **il tunnel**
Turin **Torino**
turn: turn left/right
   giri a sinistra/destra
turn signal
   la freccia, l'indicatore
   di direzione (m)
Tuscany **la Toscana**
tweezers **le pinzette**
twelve **dodici**
twenty **venti**
twin room **la camera a due**
   letti
two **due**
typewriter **la macchina da**
   scrivere

U

ugly **brutto**
umbrella **l'ombrello** (m)
uncle **lo zio**
under ... **sotto ...**
underpants **le mutande**
underskirt **la sottoveste**
understand **capire;** *I don't*
   understand **non capisco**
underwear **la biancheria**
   intima
university **l'università** (f)
university professor **il**
   professore universitario/
   la professoressa
   universitaria
unleaded **senza piombo**
until **fino a**
unusual **insolito**
up **su;** (upward) **verso l'alto;**
   up there **lassù**
urgent **urgente**
us **noi;** *it's for us* **è per noi**
use **l'uso** (m); (verb) **usare;** *it's*
   no use **non serve a niente**

useful **utile**
usual **solito**
usually **di solito**

V

vacancy (room) **la stanza libera**
vacation **la vacanza**
vaccination **la vaccinazione**
valley **la valle**
valuables **gli oggetti di valore**
valve **la valvola**
vanilla **la vaniglia**
vase **il vaso**
Vatican **il Vaticano**;
   Vatican City **la Città del Vaticano**
VCR **il videoregistratore**
veal **la carne di vitello**
vegetables **la verdura**
vegetarian **vegetariano**
vehicle **il veicolo**
Venice **Venezia**
very **molto**; *very much* **moltissimo**
vest **la canottiera**
vet **il veterinario**
video (tape/film) **il video cassetta**; *video games* **i videogiochi**
view **la vista**
viewfinder **il mirino**
villa **la villa**
village **il paese, il villaggio**
violin **il violino**
visit **la visita**; (verb) **andare a trovare**
visitor (guest) **l'ospite**
vitamin pill **la compressa di vitamine**
vodka **la vodka**
voice **la voce**; *voicemail* **la segreteria telefonica**

W

wait **aspettare**; *wait!* **aspetta!**
waiter **il cameriere**
waiting room **la sala d'aspetto**
waitress **la cameriera**
Wales **il Galles**
walk **la passeggiata**; (verb) **camminare**; *to go for a walk* **andare a fare una passeggiata**
wall **il muro**
wallet **il portafoglio**
want **volere**; *I want* (io) **voglio**

war **la guerra**
wardrobe **il guardaroba, l'armadio** (m)
warm **caldo**
was: I was (io) **ero**; *he/she/it was* (lui/lei/esso) **era**
wash (verb) **lavare**
washing machine **la lavatrice**
wasp **la vespa**
watch **l'orologio** (m); (verb) **guardare**
water **l'acqua** (f)
water heater **lo scaldabagno**
waterfall **la cascata**
wave **l'onda** (f); (verb: with hand) **salutare**
wavy: wavy hair **i capelli ondulati**
we **noi**
weather **il tempo**
website **il sito internet**
wedding **il matrimonio**
Wednesday **mercoledì**
weed **l'erbaccia** (f)
week **la settimana**
welcome **benvenuto**; *you're welcome* **di niente, prego**
well done (food) **ben cotta**
Wellington boots **gli stivali do gomma**
Welsh **gallese**
Welshman **il gallese**
Welshwoman **la gallese**
were: you were (**Lei**) **era**; (singular, familiar) (**tu**) **eri**; (plural) (**voi**) **eravate**; *we were* (**noi**) **eravamo**; *they were* (**loro**) **erano**
west **l'ovest** (m)
wet **bagnato**
what? **cosa?**
wheel **la ruota**; *wheel brace* **il girabacchino**
wheelchair **la sedia a rotelle**
when? **quando?**
where? **dove?**; *where are you from?* **di dov'è?/di dove sei?** (formal/informal)
whether **se**
which? **quale?**
white **bianco**
who? **chi?**
why? **perchè?**
wide **ampio**
wife **la moglie**
wind **il vento**
window **la finestra**

windshield **il parabrezza**
wine **il vino**; *wine list* **la lista dei vini**; *wine shop* **l'enoteca** (f)
wing **l'ala** (f)
winter **l'inverno** (m)
with **con**
withdraw (money) **prelevare**
without **senza**
witness **il/la testimone**
woman **la donna**
wood (material) **il legno**
wool **la lana**
word **la parola**
work **il lavoro**; (verb) **lavorare**; (machine) **funzionare**
worry: don't worry **non si preoccupi**
worse **peggiore**
worst **il peggiore**
wrapping paper **la carta da imballaggio**; (for presents) **la carta da regalo**
wrench **la chiave fissa**
wrist **il polso**
writing paper **la carta da scrivere**
wrong **sbagliato**

X, Y, Z

X-ray **la radiografia**
year **l'anno** (m)
yellow **giallo**
yes **sì**
yesterday **ieri**
yet **ancora**; *not yet* **non ancora**
yield **dare la precedenza**
yogurt **lo yogurt**
you: (singular, formal) **Lei**; (singular, informal) **tu**; (plural) **voi**
young **giovane**
your: (singular, formal) *your book* **il suo libro**; *your shirt* **la sua camicia**; *your shoes* **le sue scarpe**; (singular, informal) *your book* **il tuo libro**; *your shirt* **la tua camicia**; *your shoes* **le tue scarpe**
yours: is this yours? (singular, formal) **è suo?**; (singular, informal) **è tuo?**
youth hostel **l'ostello della gioventù** (m)
zipper **la chiusura lampo**
zoo **lo zoo**

DICTIONARY
Italian to English

The gender of Italian nouns listed here is indicated by the abbreviations (m) and (f), for masculine and feminine. Plural nouns are followed by the abbreviations (m pl) or (f pl). Italian adjectives (adj) vary according to the gender and number of the word they describe, and the masculine form is shown here. In general, adjectives that end in **-o** adopt an **-a** ending in the feminine form, and those that end in **-e** usually stay the same. Plural endings are **-i** for masculine and **-e** for feminine.

A

a in, at, per; **a casa** at home; **a Venezia** in Venice; **all'ufficio postale** at the post office; **alla stazione** to the station; **alle tre** at 3 o'clock; **a persona** per person; **all'anno** per annum
abbastanza enough, quite (fairly)
abbronzarsi to get a suntan
abbronzato suntanned
acceleratore (m) accelerator
accendino (m) lighter
accensione (f) ignition
acqua (f) water; **l'acqua di seltz** soda water; **l'acqua gassata** sparkling water; **l'acqua minerale** mineral water; **l'acqua naturale** still water; **l'acqua potabile** drinking water; **l'acqua tonica** tonic water
acquazzone (m) shower (rain)
adesso now
aereo (m) aircraft
aeroporto (m) airport
affare (m) business, bargain; **non sono affari tuoi** it's none of your business
affittare to rent
affollato crowded
agenda (f) planner
agente immobiliare (m/f) realtor
agenzia di viaggio (f) travel agent
aglio (m) garlic
agnello (m) lamb
ago (m) needle
agosto August
agricoltore (m) farmer
Aids AIDS
aiuola (f) flowerbed
aiutare to help
aiuto (m) help

ala (f) wing
albero (m) tree, mast; **l'albero a camme** camshaft
albicocca (f) apricot
alcol (m) alcohol
alimentari (m pl) grocery store
alla salute! cheers! (toast)
allergico allergic
alloggio (m) accommodation
allora then
le Alpi the Alps
al sangue rare (steak)
alt! stop!
alto high, tall
altro other; **l'altro** the other (one); **un altro, un'altra** another; **l'uno o l'altro** either of them; **un altro, per favore** same again, please; **qualcos'altro** something else; **qualcun'altro** someone else; **da qualche altra parte** somewhere else
alzarsi get up
amare to love
amaro bitter
ambasciata (f) embassy
ambulanza (f) ambulance
America (f) America
americano American
amico/amica (m/f) friend
ammiratore (m) fan (enthusiast)
ampio wide
ampliamento (m) enlargement
ananas (m) pineapple
anche too (also)
ancora yet; **non ancora** not yet
andare to go; **andare a trovare** to visit
anello (m) ring (jewelry)
angolo (m) corner
animato busy (bar)
anniversario (m) anniversary
anno (m) year

anticipo (m) advance (on payment, etc.); **anticipato** in advance
antiquario (m) antique shop
antisettico (m) antiseptic
aperitivo (m) aperitif
aperto open (adj)
apparecchio acustico (m) hearing aid
appartamento (m) apartment
appetito (m) appetite
appuntamento (m) appointment
apribottiglie (m) bottle opener
aprile April
aprire to open
apriscatole (m) can opener
arachidi (m pl) peanuts
arancia (f) orange (fruit)
arancione orange (color)
arazzo (m) tapestry
architettura (f) architecture
argento (m) silver (color); **d'argento** silver (metal)
aria (f) air
aria condizionata (f) air conditioning
armadio (m) cupboard, wardrobe
arrivare to arrive
arrivederci goodbye
arrivi arrivals
arrossamento (m) rash
arrosto roasted
arte (f) art
articoli per la casa (m pl) household products
artista (m/f) artist
ascensore (m) elevator
asciugamano (m) towel
asciutto dry
asmatico asthmatic
asparagi (m pl) asparagus
aspettare wait; **aspetta!** wait!

aspirina (f) *aspirin*
assegno (m) *check*
assicurazione (f) *insurance*
assomiglia a ... *it's like ...*
assorbenti (igienici) (m pl) *sanitary napkins*
attaccapanni (m) *coat hanger*
attento *careful;* **stia attento!** *be careful!*
atterrare *to land*
attraente *attractive*
attraverso *through*
aula delle lezioni (f) *lecture hall*
auricolari (m pl) *earphones*
l'Australia (f) *Australia*
australiano *Australian*
autista (m/f) *driver (of bus, truck, etc.)*
auto (m) *car*
autobus (m) *bus;* **la stazione degli autobus** *bus station;* **la fermata dell'autobus** *bus stop*
automatico *automatic*
autostop: fare l'autostop *to hitchhike*
autostrada (f) *expressway*
autunno (m) *fall, autumn*
a vapore *steamed*
avere *to have;* **non ho ...** *I don't have ...;* **ha ...?;** *do you have ...?*
avvocato (m) *lawyer*
azienda turistica (f) *tourist informaion*
azzurro *blue*

B

babbo (m) *dad*
baffi (m pl) *mustache*
bagagli (m pl) *luggage*
bagagliaio (m) *trunk (of car)*
bagaglio a mano (m) *carry-on luggage*
bagaglio in eccesso (m) *excess baggage*
bagnato *wet*
bagno (m) *bathroom;* **fare il bagno** *to take a bath;* **i bagni** *restrooms*
balcone (m) *balcony*
ballare *to dance*
ballo (m) *dance*
balsamo (m) *conditioner (hair)*
bambino (m), **bambina** (f) *baby, child*
bambola (f) *doll*
banana (f) *banana*
banca (f) *bank*
bancomat (m) *ATM*

banconota (f) *banknote*
banda (f) *band (music)*
bandiera (f) *flag*
bar (m) *bar (drinks)*
barba (f) *beard*
barbiere (m) *barber*
barca (f) *boat (small)*
basso *low, short*
basta! *enough!;* **basta così** *that'll be all*
battello (m) *boat (passenger)*
batteria (f) *battery*
baule (m) *chest (furniture)*
beige *beige*
bello *beautiful, handsome, nice*
bene *good, well;* **bene!** *good!;* **benissimo!** *great!;* **ben cotta** *well done (food);* **non mi sento bene** *I don't feel well;* **ti sta bene** *it suits you*
benvenuto *welcome*
benzina (f) *gasoline*
benzinaio (m) *gas station*
bere *to drink*
berretto (m) *cap (hat)*
biancheria (f) *laundry (dirty clothes)*
biancheria intima (f) *underwear*
bianco *white*
bibita (f) *drink*
biblioteca (f) *library*
bicchiere (m) *glass (for drinking)*
bicicletta (f) *bicycle*
bigliettaio (m) *conductor (bus)*
biglietteria (f) *ticket office, booking office*
biglietto (m) *ticket, card;* **il biglietto di andata e ritorno** *round-trip ticket;* **il biglietto di sola andata** *one-way ticket;* **il biglietto da visita** (m) *business card;* **il biglietto di auguri** *greetings card*
bigodini (m pl) *curlers*
bikini (m) *bikini*
binario (m) *platform*
biondo *blond*
birra (f) *beer*
biscotto (m) *cookie*
bisogno (m) *need;* **ho bisogno di ...** *I need ...;* **non c'è bisogno** *there's no need*
bloc-notes (m) *notepad*
blu *navy blue*
bocca (f) *mouth*
boccaglio (m) *snorkel*

bollire *to boil (water); (egg, etc.)* **far bollire**
bollitore (m) *teakettle*
borsa (f) *bag*
borsaiolo (m) *pickpocket*
borsellino (m) *purse*
botteghino (m) *box office*
bottiglia (f) *bottle*
bottone (m) *button*
braccialetto (m) *bracelet*
braccio (m) *arm*
brandy (m) *brandy*
bravo *clever*
brioche (f) *croissant*
britannico *British*
bruciare *to burn*
bruciatura (f) *burn*
brutto *ugly*
budget (m) *budget*
bunker (m) *bunker (golf)*
buonanotte *good night*
buonasera *good evening*
buongiorno *good day, hello*
buono *good, nice (to eat);* **a buon mercato** *cheap*
burro (m) *butter;* **il burro di cacao** *lip balm*
busta (f) *envelope*

C

c'è ... *there is ...;* **c'è ...?** *is there ...?*
cabina telefonica (f) *telephone booth*
cacciavite (m) *screwdriver*
caffè (m) *coffee, café;* **il caffè solubile** *instant coffee*
calcio (m) *soccer (game)*
calcolatore (m) *calculator*
caldaia (f) *boiler*
caldo *hot, warm;* **ho caldo** *I feel hot*
calzamaglia (f) *tights (wool)*
calze (f pl) *stockings*
calzini (m pl) *socks*
calzolaio (m) *shoe repairer*
cambiare *to change (money, trains)*
cambiarsi *to change (clothes)*
cambio (m) *change (money), gear (car);* **il (tasso di) cambio** *exchange rate*
camera (f) *(bed) room;* **la camera a due letti** *twin room;* **la camera doppia** *double room;* **la camera singola** *single room*
camera d'aria (f) *inner tube*
cameriera (f) *waitress, maid*
cameriere (m) *waiter*

camicetta (f) *blouse*

camicia (f) *shirt;* **la camicia da notte** *nightgown*

caminetto (m) *fireplace*

camion (m) *truck*

camminare *to walk*

campagna (f) *country (not town)*

campana (f) *bell (church)*

campanello (m) *bell (door)*

campeggio (m) *campground*

camper (m) *camper van*

campo (m) *field*

il Canada *Canada*

canadese *Canadian*

canale (m) *canal*

cancello (m) *gate*

candela (f) *candle, spark plug*

cane (m) *dog*

canoa (f) *canoe*

canottiera (f) *vest*

cantare *to sing*

cantina (f) *basement*

canzone (f) *song*

capelli (m pl) *hair*

capire *to understand;* **non capisco** *I don't understand*

capotto (m) *coat*

cappello (m) *hat*

caramella (f) *sweet*

carburatore (m) *carburetor*

caricabatterie (m) *charger*

carino *nice, pretty*

carne (f) *meat*

caro *expensive*

carota (f) *carrot*

carrello (m) *cart*

carrozzina (f) *baby carriage*

carta (f) *paper, card;* **la carta (geografica)** *map;* **la carta assegni** *debit card;* **la carta d'imbarco** *boarding card;* **la carta da** *imballaggio wrapping paper;* **la carta da regalo** *wrapping paper (for presents);* **la carta da scrivere** *writing paper;* **la carta di credito** *credit card;* **la carta igienica** *toilet paper;* **le carte da gioco** *playing cards*

cartello (m) *sign (in station, etc.)*

cartella (f) *briefcase*

cartolina (f) *postcard*

casa (f) *house, home*

cascata (f) *waterfall*

cassa (f) *checkout*

cassetta (f) *box (of wood), cassette;* **la cassetta delle lettere** *mailbox*

cassetto (m) *drawer*

cassettone (m) *chest of drawers*

cassiere (m) *cashier*

castello (m) *castle*

catenaccio (m) *bolt (on door)*

cattedrale (f) *cathedral*

cattivo *bad*

cattolico *Catholic*

cavalcavia (m) *overpass*

cavatappi (m) *corkscrew*

caviglia (f) *ankle*

cavolfiore (m) *cauliflower*

cavolo (m) *cabbage*

celibe *single (unmarried)*

cellulare (m) *cell phone*

cena (f) *supper, dinner*

cento *hundred*

centro (m) *center;* **il centro città** *downtown*

cerotto (m) *adhesive bandage*

certificato (m) *certificate*

certo *certainly*

cesoie (f pl) *shears*

cestello (m) *basket (in supermarket)*

cestino (m) *basket*

cetriolo (m) *cucumber*

check-in (m) *check-in;* **lo sportello del check-in** *check-in desk;* **fare il check-in** *to check in*

chewing gum (m) *chewing gum*

chi? *who?*

chiamare *to call*

chiaro *light (not dark), clear (obvious)*

chiave (f) *key;* **la chiave fissa** *tire iron, wrench*

chiesa (f) *church*

chilo (m) *kilo*

chilometro (m) *kilometer*

chiodo (m) *nail (metal)*

chitarra (f) *guitar*

chiudere *to close;* **chiudere con il catenaccio** *to bolt*

chiuso *closed*

chiusura lampo (f) *zipper*

ciao *hello, hi*

ciascuno *each;* **venti euro ciascuno** *twenty euros each*

cibo (m) *food*

cieco *blind (cannot see)*

cielo (m) *sky*

cifre (f pl) *figures*

ciliegia (f) *cherry*

cimitero (m) *cemetery*

cin cin! *cheers! (toast)*

cinema (m) *movie theater*

cinghia della ventola (f) *fan belt*

cinquanta *fifty*

cinque *five*

cintura (f) *belt;* **la cintura di sicurezza** *seat belt*

cioccolata (f) *chocolate;* **la scatola di cioccolatini** *box of chocolates*

ciotola (f) *bowl;* **la ciotola del cane** *dog bowl*

cipolla (f) *onion*

cipria (f) *powder (cosmetic)*

circa 16 *about 16*

ci sono *there are ...;* **ci sono?** *are there ...?*

città (f) *city, town*

ciuccio (m) *pacifier (for baby)*

clacson (m) *horn (car)*

classe (f) *class*

cliente (m) *client*

codice segreto (m) *PIN*

cofano (m) *hood (car)*

cognome (m) *last name*

coincidenza (f) *connection*

colazione (f) *breakfast*

colla (f) *glue*

collana (f) *necklace*

collant (m pl) *pantyhose*

collare (m) *collar (for dog)*

collega (m/f) *colleague*

colletto (m) *collar*

collezione (f) *collection (stamps, etc.)*

collina (f) *hill*

collo (m) *neck*

colore (m) *color*

coltello (m) *knife*

come *like;* **come questo** *like this one*

come? *how?, sorry? (pardon);* **come si chiama/ti chiami?** *what's your name? (formal/informal);* **come si chiama?** *what's it called?*

comignolo (m) *chimney*

cominciare *to start*

commedia *play (theater)*

commerciante (m/f) *shopkeeper*

comodino (m) *nightstand*

compact disc (m) *CD*

compleanno (m) *birthday;* **buon compleanno!** *happy birthday!*

completo (m) *suit*

complicato *complicated*

comprare *buy*

compressa (f) *tablet;* **la compressa di vitamine** *vitamin pill*

computer (m) *computer;*
   il computer portatile
   laptop (computer)
con *with*
concerto (m) *concert*
conchiglia (f) *shell*
conferenza (f) *lecture,*
   conference; **la sala**
   conferenze *conference*
   room
confine (m) *border*
congelatore (m) *freezer*
congratulazioni!
   congratulations!
coniglio (m) *rabbit*
conoscere *to know* (person)
consegna (f) *delivery*
consolato (m) *consulate*
consulente finanziario
   (m/f) *financial consultant*
contento *glad, happy*
conto (m) *check* (restaurant)
contraccettivo (m)
   contraceptive
contratto (m) *contract*
contro *against*
controllo (m) *test*
conversazione (f) *talk*
coperta (f) *blanket*
copriletto (m) *bedspread*
corda (f) *rope, guy rope, string*
   (guitar, etc.)
cordiale *friendly*
corno (m) *horn* (animal)
corpo (m) *body*
correre *to run*
corridoio (m) *corridor*
corrispondente (m/f) *pen pal*
corso (m) *course* (educational)
corto *short*
cosa? *what?;* **cosa c'è?** *what's*
   the matter
cosmetici (m pl) *cosmetics*
costare *to cost ;* **quanto**
   costa? *what does it cost?*
costoletta (f) *chop* (food)
costoso *expensive*
costume da bagno (m)
   swimsuit, swimming trunks
cotone (m) *cotton;* **il cotone**
   idrofilo *cotton balls*
cozze (f pl) *mussels*
crampo (m) *cramp*
cravatta (f) *tie*
crema (f) *cream, lotion*
criceto (m) *hamster*
crociera (f) *cruise*
crostacei (m pl) *shellfish*
   (crabs, etc..)
cucchiaio (m) *spoon*
cuccia (f) *dog basket*

cucina (f) *kitchen, stove*
cucinare *to cook*
cucire *to sew*
cucitrice (f) *stapler*
cugino/cugina *cousin*
cuocere (al forno) *to bake*
cuoco/cuoca (m/f) *cook*
cuoio (m) *leather*
cuore (m) *heart;* **nel cuore**
   della notte *in the middle*
   of the night
cuori (m pl) *hearts* (cards)
curry (m) *curry*
cuscino (m) *cushion*

D

dado (m) *nut* (for bolt)
dappertutto *everywhere*
dare *to give;* **dare la**
   precedenza *to yield*
davanti a *opposite, in front of*
decollo (m) *takeoff*
deliberatamente *deliberately*
denaro (m) *cash*
dente (m) *tooth*
dentiera (f) *dentures, false*
   teeth
dentifricio (m) *toothpaste*
dentista (m/f) *dentist*
denuncia (f) *statement*
   (to police)
deodorante (m) *deodorant*
desposito bagagli (m) *left*
   luggage locker
dessert (m pl) *desserts*
destro *right* (not left)
detersivo (m) *detergent;* **il**
   detersivo (per bucato)
   laundry detergent; **il**
   detersivo per i piatti
   dishwashing liquid
devo *I must;* **devo andare**
   adesso *I must go now*
di *of, from, than, on, at:* **più**
   di *more than;* **di dov'è?/**
   di dove sei? *where are*
   you from? (formal/informal);
   di lunedì *on Monday;*
   di notte *at night*
diabetico *diabetic*
diamante (m) *diamond* (gem)
diarrea (f) *diarrhea*
dica? *can I help you?*
dicembre *December*
diciannove *nineteen*
diciassette *seventeen*
diciotto *eighteen*
dieci *ten*
dietro *behind;* **dietro a ...**
   behind ...

difficile *difficult*
dimenticare *to forget*
dire *to say;* **che cosa ha**
   detto? *what did you say?;*
   come si dice ...? *how do*
   you say ...?
direttore (m) *conductor*
   (orchestra)
direttore/direttrice
   manager
direzione (f) *office*
dirigente (m) *executive*
disabili (m pl) *the disabled*
discesa per principianti (f)
   beginners' slope
disco (m) *record* (music)
dito (m) *finger*
divano (m) *sofa*
diversi *several*
diverso; è diverso! *that's*
   different!
divertente *funny*
divieto di accesso *no entry*
divorziato *divorced*
dizionario (m) *dictionary*
doccia (f) *shower*
docciaschiuma (f) *shower gel*
documento (m) *document;* **il**
   documento d'identità
   identification
dodici *twelve*
dogana (f) *customs*
dolce *sweet* (not sour)
dollaro (m) *dollar*
dolore (m) *ache, pain*
domanda (f) *question*
domani *tomorrow;* **a domani**
   see you tomorrow
domenica *Sunday*
donna (f) *woman;* **la donna**
   delle pulizie *cleaner*
dopo *after*
dopobarba (m) *aftershave*
dormire *to sleep*
dottore (m) *doctor*
dove? *where?*
due *two;* **le due** *two o'clock*
dune (f pl) *sand dunes*
duomo (m) *cathedral*
durante *during*
duro *hard*
duty free (m) *duty-free*

E

e *and;* **e poi?** *what next?*
è *he/she/it is*
eccellente *excellent*
ecco *here you are, here it is*
economico *cheap*
edificio (m) *building*

elastico (m) *elastic, rubber band*
elettricista (m/f) *electrician*
elettricità (f) *electricity*
elettrico *electric*
email (f) *email*
emergenza (f) *emergency*
enoteca (f) *wine shop*
entrare *to enter*
entrata (f) *entrance*
entro (venerdì) *by (Friday)*
epilettico *epileptic*
equipaggio (m) *crew*
era: (Lei) era *you were (singular, formal);* **(lui/lei/esso) era** *he/she/it was*
erano *they were*
eravamo *we were*
eravate *you were (plural)*
erba (f) *grass*
erbaccia (f) *weed*
eri *you were (singular, informal)*
eritema solare (m) *sunburn*
ero *I was*
errore (m) *mistake*
esatto *right (correct)*
esaurimento nervoso (m) *nervous breakdown*
esca (f) *bait*
escursione (f) *excursion*
escursionismo (m) *hiking*
esempio (m) *example;* **per esempio** *for example*
esposimetro (m) *light meter*
esso *it*
est (m) *east*
estate (f) *summer*
estintore (m) *fire extinguisher*
etichetta (f) *label*

F

faccia (f) *face*
facile *easy*
fagioli (m pl) *beans*
falegname (m) *carpenter*
falò (m) *campfire*
fame: ho fame *I'm hungry*
famiglia (f) *family*
fantastico *fantastic*
fare *to do, to make;* **che lavoro fa?** *what (work) do you do?*
fare jogging *to jog;* **andare a fare** *jogging to go jogging*
fare la fila *to line up (wait)*
fari (m pl) *lights, headlights;* **i fari posteriori** *rear lights*
farina (f) *flour*
farmacia (f) *pharmacy*

fascia (f) *bandage*
fattore di protezione (m) *SPF (sun protection factor)*
fattoria (f) *farm*
fattura (f) *invoice*
favore: per favore *please*
fazzolettini di carta (m pl) *tissues*
febbraio *February*
febbre (f) *fever, temperature*
fegato (m) *liver*
felice *happy*
felpa (f) *sweatshirt*
ferita (f) *injury*
fermare *to stop ;* **fermo!** *stop!*
fermata dell'autobus (f) *bus stop*
ferramenta (f) *hardware store*
ferro (m) *iron (metal); (for clothes)* **il ferro da stiro**
ferrovia (f) *railroad*
festa (f) *party (celebration)*
fiammifero (m) *match (light)*
fidanzata (f) *fiancée, (adj) engaged*
fidanzato (m) *fiancé, (adj) engaged*
fiera (commerciale) (f) *fair (trade)*
figlia (f) *daughter*
figlio (m) *son*
fila (f) *line, aisle (in supermarket, etc.)*
filiale (f) *branch (of company)*
film (m) *film (movies)*
filtro (m) *filter*
finalmente! *at last!*
fine (f) *end*
finestra (f) *window*
finito *finished*
fino a *until*
finocchio (m) *fennel*
fiore (m) *flower*
fiori *clubs (cards)*
Firenze *Florence*
firmare *to sign*
fissare *to arrange (appointments, etc)*
fiume (m) *river*
flash (m) *flash (camera)*
flauto (m) *flute*
flebo (f) *intravenous drip*
foglia (f) *leaf*
fohn (m) *hair dryer*
fondo (m) *bottom;* **in fondo (a)** *at the bottom (of)*
foratura (f) *puncture*
forbici (f pl) *scissors*
forchetta (f) *fork (for food)*
foresta (f) *forest*
forestiero (m) *foreigner*

formaggio (m) *cheese*
forno (m) *oven;* **il forno a microonde** *microwave*
forse *maybe, perhaps*
forte *loud, strong*
fortuna (f) *luck;* **buona fortuna!** *good luck!*
fotocopiatrice (f) *photocopier*
fotografare *to photograph*
fotografia (f) *photograph*
fotografo (m) *photographer*
foulard (m) *headscarf*
fra … *between …*
fragola (f) *strawberry*
francese *French*
la Francia *France*
francobollo (m) *stamp*
fratello (m) *brother*
frattura (f) *fracture*
freccia (f) *turn signal*
freddo *cold (adj)*
frenare *to brake*
freno (m) *brake;* **il freno a mano** *hand brake*
fresco *cool*
fretta: ho fretta *I'm in a hurry*
friggere *to fry*
frigorifero (m) *refrigerator*
fritto *fried*
frizione (f) *clutch*
frizzante *fizzy*
frutta (f) *fruit*
frutti di mare (m pl) *seafood*
fucile (m) *gun (rifle)*
fumare *to smoke*
fumatori *smoking (section);* **non fumatori** *nonsmoking*
fumo (m) *smoke*
fungo (m) *mushroom*
funivia (f) *cable car*
funzionare *to work (machine)*
fuochi d'artificio (m pl) *fireworks*
fuoco (m) *fire*
fuori *outside*
furto (m) *burglary*

G

gabbia (f) *cage*
galleria (f) *balcony (in theater);* **la galleria d'arte** *art gallery*
il Galles *Wales*
gallese *Welsh*
gamba (f) *leg*
gambero (m) *crayfish*
garage (m) *garage*
garantire *to guarantee*
garanzia (f) *guarantee*
gas *gas, fuel;* **il gas da**

campeggio *stove fuel;* **il gas per accendini** *lighter fuel*
gatto (m) *cat*
gay *gay* (homosexual)
gasolio (m) *diesel*
gel (m) *gel* (hair)
gelato (m) *ice cream*
gelo (m) *frost*
gemelli (m pl) *cufflinks*
genitori (m pl) *parents*
gennaio *January*
Genova *Genoa*
gente (f) *people*
la Germania *Germany*
ghiaccio (m) *ice*
già *already*
giacca (f) *jacket*
giallo *yellow*
giardiniere (m) *gardener*
giardino (m) *garden*
gin (m) *gin*
ginocchio (m) *knee*
giocare *to play*
giocattolo (m) *toy*
gioielliere (m) *jeweler* (shop)
giornalaio (m) *newsstand*
giornale (m) *newspaper*
giorno (m) *day;* **il giorno festivo** *public holiday*
giovane *young*
giovedì *Thursday*
girabacchino (m) *tire iron*
giri a sinistra/destra *turn left/right*
giro *tour*
giù *down*
giugno *June*
giusto *right* (correct); **non è giusto** *it's not fair*
gli *the* (m pl)
gocce (f pl) *drops*
gola (f) *throat*
golf (m) *golf*
golfista (m) *golfer*
gomito (m) *elbow*
gomma (f) *eraser, tire;* **la gomma a terra** *flat tire*
gonna (f) *skirt*
governo (m) *government*
grafico/grafica (m/f) *designer*
la Gran Bretagna *Great Britain*
granchio (m) *crab*
grande *big, large*
grande magazzino (m) *department store*
grasso (m) *fat;* *fat* (adj)
gratis *free* (no charge)
gratuito *free* (no charge)
grave *serious* (illness)
grazie *thank you/thanks*

grazioso *pretty* (beautiful)
la Grecia *Greece*
greco *Greek*
gridare *to shout*
grigio *gray*
griglia (f) *grill;* **alla griglia** *grilled*
grondaia (f) *gutter*
grotta (f) *cave*
gruppo (m) *group*
guanciale (m) *pillow*
guanti (m pl) *gloves*
guardare *to watch*
guardaroba (m) *wardrobe*
guardia (f) *guard*
guasto *breakdown* (car)
guerra (f) *war*
guida (f) *guide, guidebook;* **la guida telefonica** *telephone directory*
guidare *to drive*
guidatore/guidatrice (m/f) *driver* (car)
guinzaglio (m) *leash* (for dog)
gusto (m) *flavor*

H

ha ...? *do you have ...?*
hamburger (m) *hamburger*
HIV positivo *HIV- positive*
ho ... *I have ...*
hobby (m) *hobby*

I

i *the* (m pl)
idraulico (m) *plumber*
ieri *yesterday*
il *the* (m)
imbarazzante *embarrassing*
imbianchino (m) *decorator*
immediatamente *immediately*
immondizie (f pl) *garbage*
imparare *to learn*
impermeabile (m) *raincoat*
impiegato/impiegata (m/f) *office worker*
importa: non importa *it doesn't matter*
impossibile *impossible*
imposta (f) *shutter* (window)
in *in, to:* **in inglese** *in English;* **in Inghilterra** *to England;* **in mezzo alla piazza** *in the middle of the square;* **in centro** *to the center;* **in ritardo** *delayed*
inalatore (m) *inhaler* (for asthma, etc.)

incendio (m) *fire* (blaze)
inchiostro (m) *ink*
incidente (m) *accident*
incinta *pregnant*
incluso *included*
incontro (m) *meeting, match* (sports)
incrocio (m) *intersection*
indicatore di direzione (m) *turn signal*
indigestione (f) *indigestion*
indirizzo (m) *address;* **l'indirizzo di posta elettronica** *email address*
indistinto *faint* (unclear)
infermiere/infermiera (m/f) *nurse*
infezione (f) *infection*
informatica (f) *information technology*
informazioni (f pl) *information*
infradito (m pl) *flipflops*
ingegneria (f) *engineering*
l'Inghilterra (f) *England*
inglese *English*
ingorgo (m) *traffic jam*
iniezione (m) *injection*
inizio (m) *start*
insalata (f) *salad*
insegna (f) *sign* (road, etc.)
insegnante (m/f) *teacher*
insegnare *to teach*
insettifugo (m) *insect repellent*
insetto (m) *insect*
insieme *together*
insolito *unusual*
insonnia (f) *insomnia*
intelligente *clever*
interessante *interesting*
internet (f) *Internet*
interpretare *interpret*
interprete (m/f) *interpreter*
interruttore (m) *switch*
interurbana *long-distance* (call)
intossicazione alimentare (f) *food poisoning*
inverno (m) *winter*
invito (m) *invitation*
io *I*
l'Irlanda (f) *Ireland;* **l'Irlanda del Nord** *Northern Ireland*
irlandese *Irish*
isola (f) *island*
Italia *Italy*
italiano *Italian*

J, K

jazz (m) *jazz*
jeans (m pl) *jeans*
jogging (m) *jogging*
krapfen (m) *doughnut*

L

la *the* (f)
là *there*
lacca per i capelli (f) *hairspray*
lacci (m pl) *laces* (of shoe)
ladro (m) *burglar, thief*
laggiù *over there*
lago (m) *lake*
lamette (f pl) *razor blades*
lampada (f) *lamp;* **la lampada da studio** *reading lamp*
lampadina (f) *light bulb*
lampone (m) *raspberry*
lana (f) *wool*
lassativo (m) *laxative*
lassù *up there*
lato (m) *side* (edge)
latte (m) *milk;* **il latte detergente** *skin cleanser*
latteria (f) *dairy*
latticini (m pl) *dairy products*
lattina (f) *can* (vessel)
lattuga (f) *lettuce*
laureato: sono laureato in ... *I have a degree in ...*
lavabo (m) *sink*
lavanderia (f) *laundry* (place); **la lavanderia a secco** *dry-cleaner*
lavandino (m) *sink, wash basin*
lavastoviglie (f) *dishwasher*
lavatrice (f) *washing machine*
lavello (m) *sink* (kitchen)
lavorare *to work*
lavorare a maglia *knit*
lavoro (m) *job, work*
le *the* (f pl)
lecca lecca (m) *lollipop*
legare *to tie*
legge (f) *law*
leggere *to read*
leggero *light* (not heavy)
legno (m) *wood* (material)
lei *she*
Lei *you* (singular, formal)
lente (f) *lens;* **le lenti a contatto** *contact lenses;* **le lenti semi-rigide** *gas-permeable lenses*
lento *slow*

lenzuola (f pl) *bed linen*
lenzuolo (m) *sheet*
lesso *boiled*
lettera (f) *letter*
letteratura (f) *literature*
lettino (m) *crib*
letto (m) *bed*
leva del cambio (f) *gear stick*
levata (f) *pickup* (postal)
lezione (f) *lesson*
libbra (f) *pound* (weight)
libero *free* (not occupied)
libero professionista *self-employed*
libreria (f) *bookstore*
libretto degli assegni (m) *checkbook*
libro (m) *book*
limetta per le unghie (f) *nailfile*
limonata (f) *lemonade*
limoncello (m) *lime* (fruit)
limone (m) *lemon*
limpido *clear* (water)
linea (f) *line* (telephone, etc.); **la linea aerea** (f) *airline;* **la linea esterna** *outside line*
lingua (f) *language, tongue*
liquido per lenti (m) *soaking solution* (for contact lenses)
liquore (m) *liqueur*
lisca (f) *fishbone*
litro (m) *liter*
livido (m) *bruise*
lo *the* (m)
località sciistica (f) *ski resort*
locomotiva (f) *engine* (train)
lontano *far;* **è lontano?** *is it far away?*
loro *they, their, them;* **la loro stanza** *their room;* **il loro amico** *their friend;* **i loro libri** *their books;* **le loro penne** *their pens;* **è loro** *it's theirs;* **è per loro** *it's for them;* **dallo a loro** *give it to them*
lozione solare (f) *suntan lotion*
lucchetto (m) *padlock*
luce (f) *light*
luci di posizione (f pl) *parking lights*
lucido per le scarpe (m) *shoe polish*
luglio *July*
lui *he, him;* **è per lui** *it's for him*
luna (f) *moon;* **la luna di miele** (f) *honeymoon*
luna park (m) *fair* (funfair)

lunedì *Monday*
lunghezza (f) *length*
lungo *long*

M

ma *but*
macchina (f) *car*
macchina da scrivere (f) *typewriter*
macchina fotografica (f) *camera*
macelleria (f) *butcher shop*
madre (f) *mother*
magari *perhaps*
maggio *May*
maglieria (f) *knitwear*
maglione (m) *sweater*
magro *thin*
mai *never;* **non fumo mai** *I never smoke*
mal di denti (m) *toothache*
mal di pancia (m) *stomachache*
mal di testa (m) *headache*
malato *ill*
male: mi fa male il/la ... *my ... hurts;* **farà male?** *will it hurt?*
mamma *mom*
mancia (f) *tip* (money)
mandare *to send*
mandarino (m) *tangerine*
mangianastri (m) *cassette player*
mangiare *to eat*
manica (f) *sleeve*
maniglia (f) *handle* (door)
mano (f) *hand*
manzo (m) *beef*
marciapiede (m) *sidewalk*
mare (m) *sea*
marea (f) *tide*
margarina (f) *margarine*
marito (m) *husband*
marmellata (f) *jam;* **la marmellata d'arance** *marmalade*
marmitta (f) *exhaust* (car)
marmo (m) *marble*
marrone *brown*
martedì *Tuesday*
martello (m) *hammer*
marzo *March*
mascara (m) *mascara*
materassino gonfiabile (m) *air mattress*
materasso (m) *mattress*
matita (f) *pencil*
matrimoniale (f) *double room*

matrimonio (m) *wedding*
mattina (f) *morning;* **di mattina** *in the morning*
maturo *ripe*
meccanico (m) *mechanic*
medicina (f) *medicine*
medico (m) *doctor*
il Mediterraneo *the Mediterranean*
medusa (f) *jellyfish*
mela (f) *apple*
melone (m) *melon*
meno *less*
menta piperita (f) *peppermint*
menù (m) *menu*
mercato (m) *market*
mercoledì *Wednesday*
mese (m) *month*
messa (f) *mass* (church)
messaggio (m) *message*
metà *half*
metro (politana) (f) *subway, metro*
mettere *to put*
mezzanotte *midnight*
mezzo (f) *half:* **... e mezzo** *half past ...;* **mezz'ora** *half an hour;* **mezzo pensione** *half-board*
mezzogiorno *noon*
mia *my;* **la mia borsa** *my bag*
mi chiamo... *my name is ...*
mi dispiace *I'm sorry*
mie *my;* **le mie chiavi** *my keys*
miei *my;* **i miei vestiti** *my dresses*
miele (m) *honey*
migliore (m) *best, better;* **migliore di** *better than*
Milano *Milan*
milione *million*
mille *thousand*
minestra (f) *soup*
minuto (m) *minute*
mio *my, mine;* **il mio libro** *my book;* **è mio** *it's mine*
mirino (m) *viewfinder*
mi scusi! *excuse me!* (to get attention)
mobili (m pl) *furniture*
moda (f) *fashion*
modem (m) *modem*
modulo per la domanda (m) *application form*
moglie (f) *wife*
molla (f) *spring* (mechanical)
molletta (f) *clothespin*
molluschi (m pl) *shellfish* (mollusks)

molo (m) *dock*
molto *a lot;* **molto meglio** *much better;* **molto più lentamente** *much slower;* **non molto** *not much*
moltissimo *very much*
moneta (f) *coin*
monitor (m) *monitor* (computer)
montagna (f) *mountain*
monumento (m) *monument*
mora (f) *blackberry*
morbido *soft*
mordere *bite* (verb: by dog)
morire *to die*
morso (m) *bite* (noun: by dog)
morto *dead*
mosaico (m) *mosaic*
mosca (f) *fly* (insect)
mostra (f) *exhibition*
motocicletta (f) *motorcycle*
motore (m) *engine* (car)
motorino (m) *moped*
motoscafo (m) *motorboat*
mountain bike (m) *mountain bike*
mouse (m) *mouse* (computer)
municipio (m) *town hall*
muovere *to move;* **non muoverti!** *don't move!*
muratore (m) *builder, handyman*
muro (m) *wall*
museo (m) *museum*
musica (f) *music;* **la musica classica** *classical music;* **la musica folk** *folk music;* **la musica pop** *pop music*
musicista (m) *musician*
mutande (f pl) *underpants*

N

Napoli *Naples*
naso (m) *nose*
Natale (m) *Christmas*
nato: sono nato nel 1975 *I was born in 1975*
nave (f) *boat, ship;* **la nave a vapore** *steamer* (boat)
nebbia (f) *fog*
necessario *necessary*
negativa (f) *negative* (photo); (adj) **negativo**
negozio (m) *store, shop;* **il negozio di dischi** *record store;* **il negozio di giocattoli** (m) *toy store*
neozelandese (m/f) *New Zealander;* (adj) *New Zealand*
nero *black*

nessuno *nobody;* **da nessuna parte** *nowhere*
neve (f) *snow*
niente *nothing;* **di niente** *you're welcome;* **non serve a niente** *it's no use*
night (m) *nightclub*
nipote (f) *granddaughter, niece*
nipote (m) *grandson, nephew*
no *no* (negative response)
nocciola (f) *nut*
noce (f) *nut*
noi *we, us;* **è per noi** *it's for us*
noioso *boring;* **che noia!** *that's boring!*
noleggiare *to rent*
nome (m) *name;* **il nome di battesimo** *first name*
non *not;* **non è ...** *he's not ...*
nonna (f) *grandmother*
nonni (m pl) *grandparents*
nonno (m) *grandfather*
nord (m) *north*
normale *ordinary*
nostro/a *our;* **il nostro albergo** *our hotel;* **la nostra macchina** *our car;* **è nostro** *it's ours*
notizie (f pl) *news;* (on radio) **il notiziario**
notte (f) *night*
novanta *ninety*
nove *nine*
novembre *November*
nubile *single* (unmarried: woman)
numero (m) *number, shoe size;* **il numero di telefono** *telephone number*
nuotare *to swim*
nuoto (m) *swimming*
la Nuova Zelanda *New Zealand*
nuovo *new;* **di nuovo** *again*

O

o *or;* **o ... o ...** *either ... or ...*
obbligatorio *necessary*
occhiali (m pl) *glasses*
occhiali da sole (m pl) *sunglasses*
occhio (m) *eye;* **gli occhi** *eyes*
occupato *busy, occupied*
odore (m) *smell*
oggetti di valore (m pl) *valuables*
oggi *today*
ogni *each, every;* **ogni tanto** *occasionally*
ognuno *everyone*

olio (m) oil; olio d'oliva (m) olive oil
oliva (f) olive
ombrello (m) umbrella
ombrellone (m) sunshade
omelette (f) omelet
omeopatia homeopathy
omosessuale gay (homosexual)
onda (f) wave; i capelli ondulati (m pl) wavy hair
onesto honest
opera (f) work (of art), opera
operatore/operatrice (m/f) operator
operazione (f) operation
opuscolo (m) brochure
ora (f) hour; ora sono occupato I'm busy now
orario (m) schedule, timetable; l'orario di apertura opening times; l'orario di visita (m) visiting hours
orchestra (f) orchestra
ordinativo (m) order (for goods)
ordine del giorno (m) agenda
ore: che ore sono? what's the time?
orecchini (m pl) earrings
orecchio (m) ear; le orecchie ears
organo (m) organ (music)
oro (m) gold
orologio (m) clock, watch
orribile awful, horrible
ospedale (m) hospital
ospite (m/f) guest
ossigenare to bleach (hair)
osso (m) bone
ostello della gioventù (m) youth hostel
ottanta eighty
ottico (m) optician
ottimo excellent
otto eight
ottobre October
otturatore (m) shutter (camera)
otturazione (f) filling (in tooth)
ovest (m) west

P

pacchetto (m) package, packet
pacco (m) parcel
padella (f) frying pan
Padova Padua

padre (m) father
padrona di casa (f) hostess
padrone di casa (m) host
paese (m) country (state), village
pagamento (m) payment
pagare to pay; pagare in contanti to pay cash
pagina (f) page
paio (m) pair
palazzo (m) palace
palestra (f) gymnastics
palla (f) ball (soccer, etc.)
pallido pale
pallina (f) ball (tennis, etc.)
pallone (m) ball, soccer ball
palo della tenda (m) tent pole
pancetta (f) bacon
pane (m) bread; il pane tostato (m) toast
panetteria (f) bread shop
panino (m) sandwich; rock (music)
panna (f) cream (dairy)
pannolini (m pl) diapers
pantaloncini corti (m pl) shorts
pantaloni (m pl) pants, trousers
pantofole (m pl) slippers
papà (m) dad
Papa: il Papa Pope
parabrezza (m) windshield
paraffina (f) kerosene
paralume (m) lampshade
paraurti (m) bumper
parcheggiare to park
parcheggio (m) parking lot
parco (m) park
parlare to talk, speak; parla ...? do you speak ...?; non parlo ... I don't speak ...
parola (f) word
parrucchiere (m) hair salon
parte posteriore (f) back (not front)
partenza (f) departure; le partenze departures
particolarmente especially
partire to depart, leave
partito (m) party (political)
passaporto (m) passport; il controllo passaporti passport control
passatempo (m) hobby
passeggero/passeggera (m/f) passenger
passeggiata (f) walk; andare a fare una passeggiata to go for a walk

passegino (m) pushchair
password (f) password
pasta (f) pasta
pasticceria (f) bakery
pasticche per la gola (f pl) throat lozenges
pasto (m) meal
patata (f) potato
patatine (f pl) chips
patatine fritte (f) french fries
patente (f) license; patente di guida driver's license
patio (m) terrace
pattini da ghiaccio (m pl) ice skates
pattumiera (f) garbage can
paura: ho paura I'm frightened
pavimento (m) floor (ground)
pazzo crazy
pedone (m) pedestrian; la zona pedonale pedestrian zone
peggiore worst, worse
pelle (f) leather
pelletteria (f) leather goods shop
pellicola (f) film (for camera)
penicillina (f) penicillin
penna (f) pen
pennello (m) paintbrush
pensare to think; penso di sì I think so; ci penserò I'll think about it
pensione completa (f) full board
pentola (f) saucepan; la pentola a pressione steamer (for cooking)
pepe (m) pepper (spice)
peperone (m) pepper (red, green)
per for; per me for me
pera (f) pear
perché because
perché? why?, what for?
perfetto perfect
pericoloso dangerous
periferia (f) suburbs
perla (f) pearl
permanente (f) perm
permesso allowed; permesso! excuse me! (to get past)
persiane (f pl) shutters (window)
pesante heavy
pesca (f) peach, fishing; andare a pesca to go fishing
pesce (m) fish

pescheria (f) *fishmonger* (shop)
pettinare *to comb*
pettine (m) *comb*
petto (m) *chest* (part of body)
pezzi di ricambio (m pl) *spare parts* (car)
pezzo (m) *piece*
piace: mi piace ... *I like ...;* **mi piace nuotare** *I like swimming*
piacere *pleased to meet you*
piacere di conoscerla *how do you do?*
piangere *cry* (verb: weep)
piano (m) *floor* (story); **piano di lavoro** *countertop*
pianta (f) *map* (of town), *plan; plant*
pianterreno (m) *ground floor*
piastrella (f) *tile*
piattino (m) *saucer*
piatto (m) *plate, meal;* **i piatti pronti** *prepared meals*
piatto *flat* (level)
piazza (f) *square*
piazzola (f) *site* (in campground, etc.)
picche (m pl) *spades* (cards)
picchetto (m) *tent peg*
piccolo *little, small*
picnic (m) *picnic*
piede (m) *foot;* **a piedi** *on foot*
pieno *full*
pigiama (m) *pajamas*
pigro *lazy*
pin (m) *PIN*
pinacoteca (f) *art gallery*
pinne (f pl) *flippers*
pinzette (f pl) *tweezers*
pioggia (f) *rain*
piovra (f) *octopus*
pipa *pipe* (for smoking)
piscina (f) *swimming pool*
piselli (m pl) *peas*
pistola (f) *gun* (**pistol**)
pistone (m) *piston*
pittura (f) *painting*
più *more;* **più di ...** *more than ...;* **più presto possibile** *as soon as possible*
piumino (m) *comforter*
piuttosto *pretty, quite*
pizzo (m) *lace*
plastica (f) *plastic*
platea (f) *orchestra* (in theater)
po' *a little;* **è un po' grande** *it's a little big;* **solo un po'** *just a little*
poi *then*

polipo (m) *octopus*
politica (f) *politics*
polizia (f) *police*
poliziotto (m) *police officer*
pollame (m) *poultry*
pollo (m) *chicken*
polso (m) *wrist*
poltrona (f) *armchair*
pomata (f) *ointment*
pomeriggio (m) *afternoon*
pomodoro (m) *tomato*
ponte (m) *bridge*
porcellana (f) *china*
porta (f) *door*
portacenere (m) *ashtray*
portafoglio (m) *wallet*
portare *to bring;* **da portare via** *to carry out*
portiere (m) *porter* (hotel); **il portiere di notte** *night porter*
portinaio/portinaia *caretaker*
porto (m) *harbor, port*
possibile *possible*
posso avere ...? *can I have ...?*
posta (f) *mail;* **la posta elettronica** *email*
posteggio dei taxi (m) *taxi stand*
postino (m) *mail carrier*
posto (m) *place, accommodation, seat*
postumi della sbornia (m pl) *hangover*
potreste ...? *can you ...?*
povero *poor*
pranzo (m) *lunch*
prato (m) *lawn*
preferire *to prefer*
prego *you're welcome;* **prego?** *pardon?*
prelevare *to withdraw* (money)
prendere *to fetch* (something)
prendere *to take;* **prendere il sole** *to sunbathe;* **prendere il treno** *to catch the train*
prenotare *to book*
prenotazione (f) *reservation*
preoccupi: non si preoccupi *don't worry*
presa di corrente (f) *electrical hookup*
preservativo (m) *condom*
presto *early;* **a presto** *see you soon*
prete (m) *priest*
preventivo (m) *estimate*

prezzemolo (m) *parsley*
prezzo (m) *price;* **il prezzo d'ingresso** *admission charge*
prima di ... *before ...*
primavera (f) *spring* (season)
primi piatti (m pl) *appetizers*
primo *first;* **il primo piano** *second floor;* **la prima classe** *first class*
principiante (m/f) *beginner*
privato *private*
problema (m) *problem;* **non c'è problema** *no problem*
professore/professoressa (m/f) *teacher;* **il professore universitario** *university lecturer*
profitti (m pl) *profits*
profondo *deep*
profumo (m) *perfume*
proibito *forbidden*
prolunga (f) *extension cord*
pronto *ready, hello* (on phone)
pronto soccorso (m) *emergency department, first aid*
prosciutto (m) *ham*
prossimo *next;* **la settimana prossima** *next week*
provare *to try*
pubblico *public*
pulce (f) *flea*
pulire *to clean*
pulito *clean* (adj)
pullman (m) *long-distance bus*
pungere *to bite* (by insect)
punta (f) *tip* (end)
puntina da disegno (f) *thumbtack*
puntura (f) *bite* (by insect)
può *he/she can;* **non può ...** *he/she can't ...*
puzzare *to smell* (stink)

Q

quaderno (m) *notebook*
quadrato *square* (adj: shape)
quadri (m pl) *diamonds* (cards)
qualche modo *somehow*
qualche parte *somewhere*
qualche volta *sometimes*
qualcosa *something*
qualcuno *somebody*
quale? *which?*
qualità (f) *quality*
quando? *when?*
quant'è? *how much is that?*
quanti anni hai? *how old are you?*

quanto ci vuole? *how long does it take?*

quanto costa? *how much?*

quanto dista da qui …? *how far is it to …?*

quaranta *forty*

quarto (m) *quarter; … e un quarto quarter past …*

quarto *fourth*

quasi *almost*

quattordici *fourteen*

quattro *four*

quei *those;* **quei ragazzi** *those boys*

quella *that;* **quella donna** *that woman*

quelle *those;* **quelle cose** *those things*

quelli *those;* **prendo quelli** *I'll take those*

quello *that;* **quell'uomo** *that man;* **cos'è quello?** *what's that?*

questa *this;* **questa donna** *this woman*

queste *these;* **queste cose** *these things*

questi *these;* **questi ragazzi** *these boys*

questo *this;* **questo quadro** *this picture;* **quest'uomo** *this man;* **cos'è questo?** *what's this?;* **questo è il signor …** *this is Mr …*

quindici *fifteen*

R

raccomandata *registered (mail)*

radersi *to shave*

radiatore (m) *radiator*

radio (f) *radio*

radiografia (f) *X-ray*

raffreddore (m) *cold (illness);* **ho un raffreddore** *I have a cold*

ragazza (f) *girl*

ragazzo (m) *boy*

ragioniere/ragioniera (m/f) *accountant*

ragno (m) *spider*

rapporto di polizia (m) *police report*

raro *rare (uncommon)*

rastrello (m) *rake*

ratto (m) *rat*

ravanello (m) *radish*

reception (f) *reception (hotel)*

receptionist (m/f) *receptionist*

record (m) *record (sports, etc.)*

regalo (m) *gift*

reggiseno (m) *bra*

relazione (f) *report*

religione (f) *religion*

remare *to row*

remi (m pl) *oars*

rene (m) *kidney*

reparto (m) *department, ward;* **il reparto di pediatria** *children's ward*

respirare *to breathe*

resti (m pl) *ruins*

restituire *to return (give back)*

resto (m) *rest (noun: remainder)*

reticella (per i bagagli) (f) *luggage rack*

riavere indietro qualcosa *to get something back*

ribes nero (m) *black currant*

ricci (m pl) *curls*

ricco *rich*

ricerca (f) *research*

ricetta (f) *prescription*

ricevere *to get (obtain)*

ricevuta (f) *receipt (restaurants, hotels)*

ricordare *to remember;* **non ricordo** *I don't remember*

ridere *to laugh*

riduttore (m) *adapter*

riduzione (f) *discount*

rifiuti (m pl) *litter (trash can)*

riga (f) *ruler (for drawing)*

rilassarsi *to relax*

rimorchio (m) *trailer*

rinfreschi (m pl) *refreshments*

rinfresco *reception (party)*

ringraziare *to thank*

riparare *to repair*

ripieno (m) *filling (in sandwich, cake, etc.)*

riposarsi *to rest*

riscaldamento (m) *heating;* **il riscaldamento centrale** *central heating*

riscuotere *to cash*

riso (m) *rice*

ristorante (m) *restaurant*

ritardo: l'autobus è in ritardo *the bus is late*

ritiro bagagli (m) *baggage claim*

ritornare *to return*

riunione (f) *meeting*

rivista (f) *magazine*

roccia *rock (stone)*

Roma *Rome*

romanzo (m) *novel*

rosa (f) *rose; pink (color)*

rossetto (m) *lipstick*

rosso *red*

rotatoria (f) *roundabout*

rotondo *round (circular)*

rotto *broken;* **la gamba rotta** *broken leg*

roulotte (f) *trailer, camper trailer*

rovine (f pl) *ruins*

rubare *steal;* **è stato rubato** *it's been stolen*

rubinetto (m) *tap*

rubino (m) *ruby (gem)*

rugby (m) *rugby*

rullino a colori (m) *color film*

rum (m) *rum*

rumoroso *noisy*

ruota (f) *wheel*

ruscello (m) *stream*

S

sabato *Saturday*

sabbia (f) *sand*

sacchetto (m) *bag;* **il sacchetto di plastica** (m) *plastic bag;* **il sacchetto per la pattumiera** (m) *garbage bag*

sacco a pelo (m) *sleeping bag*

sala (f) *room;* **la sala d'aspetto** *waiting room;* **la sala da pranzo** *dining room;* **la sala operatoria** *operating room*

salame (m) *salami*

saldi (m pl) *sale (at reduced prices)*

sale (m) *salt*

salire *to go up;* **salire su** *to get on (bus, etc.)*

salmone (m) *salmon*

salsa (f) *sauce*

salsiccia (f) *sausage*

salumeria (f) *delicatessen*

salutare *to wave*

sandali (m pl) *sandals*

sangue (m) *blood;* **le analisi del sangue** *blood test*

sapere *know (fact);* **I don't know non so**

sapone (m) *soap*

la Sardegna *Sardinia*

sauna (f) *sauna*

sazio *full (up):* **sono sazio** *I'm full (after a meal)*

sbagliato *wrong*
sbrigati! *hurry up!*
scacchi (m pl) *chess*
scala (f) *staircase;* **le scale**
stairs; **la scala mobile**
escalator
scaldabagno (m) *water*
heater
scambiare *to exchange*
scarpe (f pl) *shoes;* **le scarpe**
da ginnastica *athletic*
shoes
scatola (f) *box, tin*
scendere *to go down;*
scendere da *to get off*
(bus, etc.)
scheda telefonica (f)
phonecard
schermo (m) *screen*
scherzo (m) *joke*
schiena (f) *back* (body)
schiuma (f) *foam, mousse,*
cream (for hair); **la schiuma**
da barba *shaving cream*
sci (m pl) *skis*
scialle (m) *shawl*
sciare: andare a sciare
to go skiing
sciarpa (f) *scarf*
scienza (f) *science*
sciroppo (m) *syrup*
scodella (f) *bowl*
scompartimento (m)
compartment
scontrino (m) *receipt*
(shops, bars)
scopa (f) *brush* (cleaning)
la Scozia *Scotland*
scozzese *Scottish*
scritto da ... *written by ...*
scrivania (f) *desk*
scuola (f) *school*
scuro *dark*
scusate! *excuse me!* (when
sneezing, etc.)
scusi! *sorry!;* **scusi?** *pardon?*
se *if, whether*
secchio (m) *bucket*
secco *dry* (wine)
secondi piatti (m pl)
main courses
secondo *second;* **seconda**
classe *second class*
sede centrale (f)
headquarters
sedia (f) *chair;* **la sedia**
girevole *swivel chair;* **la**
sedia a rotelle *wheelchair*
sedici *sixteen*
seggiolino per macchina
(m) *car seat* (for a baby)

segretario/segretaria (m/f)
secretary; **la segreteria**
telefonica *answering*
machine; **la segreteria**
telefonica *voicemail*
sei *six*
sei *you are* (singular, informal)
semaforo (m) *traffic lights*
seminario (m) *seminar*
seminterrato (m) *basement*
semplice *simple*
sempre *always;* **sempre**
dritto *straight ahead*
senape (f) *mustard*
senso unico *one way*
sentiero (m) *path*
sentire *to hear*
senza *without;* **senza**
piombo *unleaded*
separati *separated* (couple)
separato *separate* (adj)
sera (f) *evening*
serio *serious*
servizio in camera (m)
room service
sessanta *sixty*
seta (f) *silk*
sete *thirsty;* **ho sete** *I'm*
thirsty
settanta *seventy*
sette *seven*
settembre *September*
settimana (f) *week;* **la**
settimana scorsa
last week
shampoo (m) *shampoo*
sherry (m) *sherry*
shopping *shopping*
short (m pl) *shorts*
sì *yes*
sia ... che ... *both ... and ...*
siamo *we are*
la Sicilia *Sicily*
sicuro *safe* (not dangerous);
sure (certain); **sei sicuro?**
are you sure?
siepe (f) *hedge*
siete *you are* (plural, informal)
sigaretta (f) *cigarette*
sigaro (m) *cigar*
significa: che cosa
significa? *what does*
this mean?
Signor *Mr.*
signora (f) *lady, madam;*
Signora *Mrs.*
signore *sir*
Signorina *Miss*
simpatico *nice* (pleasant)
sinagoga (f) *synagogue*
sinistra *left* (not right)

sito internet (m) *website*
slittare *to skid*
smalto per le unghie (m)
nail polish
soffitta (f) *attic*
soffitto (m) *ceiling*
soffocante *stuffy*
soggiorno (m) *living room*
soldi (m pl) *money*
sole (m) *sun;* **c'è il sole** *it's*
sunny
solito *usual;* **di solito** *usually*
sollievo: che sollievo! *what*
a relief!
solo *alone, single* (one), *only;*
da solo *by oneself*
sonnifero (m) *sleeping pill*
sonno (m) *sleep*
sono *I am;* **sono di ...**
I come from ...
sopra *over* (above)
sopracciglio (m) *eyebrow*
sordo *deaf*
sorella (f) *sister*
sorpassare *to pass* (driving)
sorridere *to smile*
sorriso (m) *smile*
sosta vietata *no parking*
sotto *below, under*
sottoveste (f) *underskirt*
souvenir (m) *souvenir*
la Spagna *Spain*
spagnolo *Spanish*
spago *string* (cord)
spalla (f) *shoulder*
spazio (m) *room* (space)
spazzatura (f) *garbage*
spazzola (f) *hairbrush*
spazzolare *to brush* (hair)
spazzolino da denti (m)
toothbrush
specchio (m) *mirror*
spedire per posta *to mail*
spesa (f) *shopping;* **andare**
a fare la spesa *to*
go shopping
spesso *often; thick*
spettatori *audience*
spiacente *I'm sorry*
spiaggia (f) *beach*
spicci (m pl) *cash, change*
spilla (f) *brooch;* **la spilla**
di sicurezza *safety pin*
spillatrice (f) *stapler*
spina *plug* (electrical)
spinaci (m pl) *spinach*
spingere *to push*
sporco *dirty*
sport (m) *sports*
sportello (m) *door* (of car); **lo**
sportello automatico *ATM*

sposato *married*
spuntino (m) *snack*
stampante (f) *printer*
stampelle (f pl) *crutches*
stanco *tired*
stanza (f) *room;* **stanza libera** *vacancy (room)*
star (f) *star (film)*
stasera *tonight*
statua (f) *statue*
stazione (f) *station;* **la stazione di polizia** *police station;* **la stazione di servizio** (f) *gas station*
steccato (m) *fence*
stella (f) *star*
stereo (m) *music system*
sterlina (f) *pounds sterling*
stesso *same;* **lo stesso vestito** *the same dress*
stirare *to iron*
stivale (m) *boot (footwear);* **gli stivali do gomma** *Wellington boots*
stoffa (f) *fabric*
stomaco (m) *stomach*
storia (f) *history*
straccio per la polvere (m) *duster*
strada (f) *road, street*
straniero (m) *foreigner*
strano *odd, funny*
stretta di mano (f) *handshake*
stretto *narrow, tight (clothes)*
strofinaccio (m) *dishcloth*
strumento musicale (m) *musical instrument*
studente/studentessa (m/f) *student*
stupido *stupid*
su *on, over (above);* **sul tavolo** *on the table;* **un libro su Venezia** *a book on Venice*
succo (m) *juice;* **il succo d'arancia** *orange juice;* **il succo di frutta** *fruit juice;* **il succo di pomodoro** *tomato juice*
sud (m) *south*
sudare *to sweat*
sudore (m) *sweat*
suo *her/his/your (singular, formal):* **il suo libro** *her/his/your book;* **la sua casa** *her/his/your house;* **le sue scarpe** *her/his/your shoes;* **i suoi vestiti** *her/his/your dresses;* **è suo** *it's hers/his/yours*
suoceri (m pl) *in-laws*

supermercato (m) *supermarket*
supplemento *supplement*
supposta (f) *suppository*
surgelati (m pl) *frozen foods*
sveglia (f) *alarm clock*
svenire *to faint*
sviluppare *to develop (film)*
la Svizzera *Switzerland*
svizzero *Swiss*

T

tabaccaio (m) *tobacconist's (shop)*
tabacco (m) *tobacco*
tacco (m) *heel (of shoe)*
taglia (f) *size (clothes)*
tagliare *to cut, chop*
tagliaunghie (m) *nail clippers*
taglio (m) *cut, haircut*
talco (m) *talcum powder*
tallone (m) *heel (of foot)*
tamponi (m pl) *tampons*
tappeto (m) *carpet, rug*
tappo (m) *cap (bottle), cork, plug (sink)*
tardi *late;* **si sta facendo tardi** *it's getting late;* **più tardi** *later*
targa (f) *license plate*
tariffa (f) *fare, rate;* **la tariffa ridotta** (f) *discount rate*
tasca (f) *pocket*
tastare *to feel (touch)*
tastiera (f) *keyboard*
tavoletta di cioccolata (f) *bar of chocolate*
tavolo (m) *table*
taxi (m) *taxi*
tazza (f) *cup*
tazzone (m) *mug*
tè (m) *tea;* **il tè con latte** *tea with milk*
teatro (m) *theater*
tecnico (m) *technician*
tedesco *German*
telefonare *to telephone*
telefonata (f) *telephone call*
telefonino (m) *cell phone*
telefono (m) *telephone*
televisione (f) *television*
telo protettivo (m) *flysheet*
telone impermeabile (m) *groundsheet*
temperamatite (m) *pencil sharpener*
temperatura (f) *temperature*
temperino (m) *penknife*

tempesta (f) *storm*
tempo (m) *time, weather;* **il tempo libero** *leisure time*
temporale (m) *thunderstorm*
tenda (f) *curtain, tent;* **la tenda avvolgibile** *blind (on window)*
tennis (m) *tennis*
terminale (m) *terminal (airport)*
termosifone (m) *heater*
terra (f) *soil, land*
terribile *awful, terrible*
terrina (f) *mixing bowl*
terzo *third*
testa (f) *head*
testimone (m/f) *witness*
tetto (m) *roof*
il Tevere *the Tiber*
tirare *to pull*
tisana (f) *herbal tea*
toilette (f) *toilet;* (men's room) **la toilette degli uomini;** (ladies' room) **la toilette delle donne**
topo (m) *mouse (animal)*
torcia (elettrica) (f) *flashlight*
Torino *Turin*
tornare *to come back*
torre (f) *tower*
torta (f) *cake*
tosaerba (m) *lawnmower*
la Toscana *Tuscany*
tosse (f) *cough*
tossire *to cough*
tovagliolo (m) *napkin*
tradizione (f) *tradition*
tradurre *to translate*
traduttore/traduttrice (m/f) *translator*
traffico (m) *traffic*
traghetto (m) *ferry*
trampolino (m) *diving board*
tranquillo *quiet*
traslocare *to move (to new house)*
trattore (m) *tractor*
tre *three*
trecento *three hundred*
tredici *thirteen*
treno (m) *train*
trenta *thirty*
triste *sad*
troppo *too (excessively)*
trucco (m) *makeup*
tu *you (singular, informal)*
tubo (m) *hose, pipe (for water)*
tuffarsi *to dive*
tuffo (m) *dive (noun)*
tunnel (m) *tunnel*

tuo *your (singular, informal);*
   il tuo libro *your book;*
   la tua camicia *your shirt;*
   le tue scarpe *your shoes;*
   è tuo? *is this yours?*
turista (m/f) *tourist*
tutto *all;* **tutto** *everything;*
   tutte le strade *all*
   the streets; **questo è**
   tutto *that's all;* **tutti**
   everyone; **tutti i giorni**
   every day
TV cavo *cable TV*
TV satellite *satellite TV*

U

ubriaco *drunk*
uccello (m) *bird*
udire *to hear*
ufficio (m) *office;* **l'ufficio**
   oggetti smarriti *lost*
   property office; **l'ufficio**
   postale *post office;* **l'ufficio**
   turistico *tourist office*
ultimo *last (final)*
umido *damp*
un/uno/una/un' *a*
undici *eleven*
unghia (f) *nail (finger)*
unguento (m) *ointment*
università (f) *university*
uno *one;* **l'una** *one o'clock*
uomo (m) *man;* **gli uomini**
   men
uovo (m) *egg*
urgente *urgent*
usare *to use*
uscire *to go out*
uscita (f) *exit, gate (at airport)*
uso (m) *use*
utile *useful*
uva (f) *grapes*
uvetta (f) *raisins*

V

vacanza (f) *vacation*
vaccinazione (f) *vaccination*
vagone letto (m) *sleeper car*

valigia (f) *case,*
   suitcase
valle (f) *valley*
valvola (f) *valve*
vanga (f) *spade (shovel)*
vaniglia (f) *vanilla*
varecchina (f) *bleach*
vasca (f) *bathtub*
vaso (m) *vase*
vassoio (m) *tray*
vattene! *go away!*
il Vaticano *Vatican;*
   la Città del Vaticano
   Vatican City
vecchio *old*
vedere *to see*
vegetariano *vegetarian*
veicolo (m) *vehicle*
vela (f) *sailing*
veleno (m) *poison*
veloce *fast, quick*
velocità (f) *speed*
vendere *to sell*
vendite (f pl) *sales*
   (of goods, etc.)
venerdì *Friday*
Venezia *Venice*
venga qui! *come here!*
   (informal); **venga**
   con me *come with*
   me (informal)
venire *to come*
venti *twenty*
ventilatore (m) *fan*
   (ventilator)
vento (m) *wind*
verde *green*
verdura (f) *vegetables*
vernice (f) *paint*
vero *true*
vespa (f) *wasp*
vestito (m) *dress;* **i vestiti**
   clothes
veterinario (m) *vet*
vetro (m) *glass (material)*
via aerea *air mail*
viaggiare *to travel*
viaggio (m)
   jtrip, *journey*
viale (m) *driveway*

vialetto (m) *path*
vieni qui! *come here! (formal);*
   vieni con me *come with*
   me (formal)
vicino (a) *close, near (to);*
   vicino alla finestra *near*
   the window; **vicino alla**
   porta *near the door*
video cassetta (m) *video*
   (tape/film)
videogiochi (m pl) *video*
   games
videoregistratore (m) *VCR*
villa (f) *villa*
villaggio (m) *village*
vino (m) *wine;* **la lista dei**
   vini *wine list*
viola *purple*
violino (m) *violin*
visita (f) *visit;* **la visita**
   guidata *guided tour*
vista (f) *view*
vita (f) *life, screw*
vivaio (m) *garden center*
vocabolarietto (m)
   phrasebook
voce (f) *voice*
vodka (f) *vodka*
voi *you (plural)*
volantino (m) *leaflet*
volare *to fly*
volere *to want*
volo (m) *flight;* **il numero**
   del volo *flight number*
vorrei *I'd like*
vuoto *empty*

W, Y, Z

whisky (m) *whisky*
yogurt (m) *yogurt*
zaino (m) *backpack*
zanzara (f) *mosquito*
zenzero (m) *ginger*
   (spice)
zia (f) *aunt*
zio (m) *uncle*
zoo (m) *zoo*
zucchero (m) *sugar*
zuppa (f) *soup*

Acknowledgments

The publisher would like to thank the following for their help in the preparation of this book: Fiorella Elviri and Anna Mazzotti for the organization of location photography in Italy; Farmacia Gaoni, Rome; La Taverna dei Borgia, Rome; Treni Italia, Tuscolana, Rome; Coolhurst Tennis Club, London; Magnet Showroom, Enfield, MyHotel, London; Kathy Gammon; Juliette Meeus and Harry.

Language content for Dorling Kindersley by **g-and-w publishing**
Managed by **Jane Wightwick**
Editing and additional input: **Paula Tite**

Additional design assistance: **Phil Gamble, Lee Riches, Fehmi Cömert, Sally Geeve**
Additional editorial assistance: **Kajal Mistry, Paul Docherty, Nikki Sims, Lynn Bresler**
Picture research: **Louise Thomas**

Picture credits

Key: *t=top; b=bottom; l=left, r=right; c=centre; A=above; B=below*

p2 **DK Images:** *Demetrio Carrasco; p4/5* **DK Images:** *Max Alexander trl Demetrio Carrasco bl; p6/7* **Laura Knox:** *cl; p10/11* **Alamy:** *BananaStock cAr; RubberBall cBl, bl;* **Ingram Image Library:** *bl; p12/13* **Alamy:** *John Foxx cl, cAr; RubberBall br;* **DK Images:** *Steve Shott cBr;* **Ingram Image Library:** *tr, cr; p14/15* **Alamy:** *Comstock Images tcr; Think Stock bcl;* **Dreamstime.com:** *Slobodan Mračina (cl);* **Ingram Image Library:** *cAl, cl, cBl, cAr, cBr, bcr; p16/17* **Alamy:** *Think Stock crA;* **Getty:** *Taxi / James Day bcr;* **Ingram Image Library:** *tr; p18/19* **DK Images:** *David Murray tr; p22/23* **DK Images:** *cl, Andy Crawford cAr; Susanna Price br; Magnus Rew tcrB;* **Ingram Image Library:** *bcl, tcr; p24/25* **DK Images:** *clA, Dave King tcr; p26/27* **Ingram Image Library:** *cl; p28/29* **DK Images:** *John Bulmer tcr; Dave King cr; Matthew Ward bclA;* **Ingram Image Library:** *bcrA, bcr; p30/31* **Alamy:** *Comstock Images bcl;* **DK Images:** *cl; 34/35* **Dreamstime.com:** *Slobodan Mračina (cb); p36/37* **DK Images:** *bcl, bcr; Magnus Rew cl;* **Dreamstime.com:** *Slobodan Mračina (cla);* **Ingram Image Library:** *bl;* **iStockphoto.com:** *nicolas_ (cla/sim card); p38/39* **Alamy:** *Imageshop / Zefa Visual Media cl; p40/41* **DK:** *Sean Hunter cl; p42/43* **DK:** *Demetrio Carrasco cAAr; Mike Dunning tcr; p44/45 Courtesy of* **Renault:** *c; p46/47* **Alamy:** *Imageshop / Zefa Visual Media br;* **DK Images:** *Sean Hunter bcl;* **Ingram Image Library:** *tclB; Courtesy of* **Renault:** *tcr; p48/49* **Alamy:** *CuboImages cAl;* **DK Images:** *Max Alexander bcl; Kim Sayer c, cl; p50/51* **Alamy:** *Robert Harding Picture Library c; Peter Titmuss cr; p52/53* **Alamy:** *Image Farm Inc cAr;* **DK Images:** *cl; p54/55* **Alamy:** *Frank Herholdt bcl; Jackson Smith cBl;* **Alamy:** *BananaStock cl; John Foxx c; Image Source cAr; ThinkStock tcr;* **DK Images:** *Andy Crawford bclA; p56/57* **Alamy:** *CuboImages tcll;* **DK Images:** *Max Alexander clAA; Kim Sayer cAl, c; Courtesy of* **Renault:** *bc; p58/59* **Alamy:** *Michael Juno tcr;* **Alamy:** *Brand X Pictures cBl, cBBl; Image Source cAAl;* **DK Images:** *cAl; p60/61* **123RF.com:** *shutswis (cb);* **Alamy:** *Robert Harding Picture Library bcr;* **Alamy:** *Image Source cAr; Barry Mason bl;* **DK Images:** *Steve Gorton tcrB; Pia Tryde cAAr;* **Ingram Image Library:** *cr; p62/63* **DK Images:** *Stephen Whitehorn c; p64/65* **Alamy:** *Arcaid bcrA;* **Alamy:** *GKPhotography cBr; Goodshoot cAAr; Justin Kase tcrB;* **DK Images:** *Roger Moss c; Steve Tanner cAr;* **Ingram Image Library:** *tcr; p66/67* **Alamy:** *Arcaid tl;* **Alamy:** *Image Source cAr;* **DK Images:** *tr; Stephen Whitehorn bl;* **Ingram Image Library:** *br; p68/69* **Alamy:** *Balearic Pictures cr; p72/73* **Alamy:** *imagebroker tcrB; Image Source cAr; Comstock Images tcr;* **Avery Weight-Tronix:** *bl; p74/75* **Alamy RF:** *Doug Norman bl;* **Ingram Image Library:** *c; p76/77* **Alamy:** *Balearic Pictures cBl; p78/79* **Alamy:** *Think Stock bcr; p80/81* **Getty:** *Taxi / Rob Melnychuk bc;* **Ingram Image Library:** *cAr; Xerox UK Ltd:* *tcr; p82/83* **Alamy:** *wildphotos.com tcr;* **Alamy:** *FogStock cAAl; Momentum Creative Group cAl; Shoosh / Up the Res cBl;* **Ingram Image Library:** *cl; p84/85* **Alamy:** *Brand X Pictures cr; f1 Online c;* **Alamy RF:** *BananaStock bl; SuperStock tr;* **Ingram Image Library:** *crB; p86/87* **Alamy:** *Luca DiCecco bcl;* **Getty:** *Taxi / Rob Melnychuk tc; p90/91* **Alamy:** *Brand X Pictures tcr;* **DK Images:** *cl; David Jordan cAr; Stephen Oliver cr;* **Ingram Image Library:** *cBr; p92/93* **Alamy:** *Pixland cr;* **DK Images:** *cl; Guy Ryecart tcr; p94/95* **Alamy:** *David Kamm cl; Phototake Inc bcl;* **Alamy:** *Comstock Images cr; ImageState Royalty Free bcr;* **DK Images:** *Stephen Oliver tcr; p96/97* **Alamy:** *Pixland br;* **DK Images:** *tl;* **Ingram Image Library:** *tr; p98/99* **Alamy:** *Shotfile cr;* **Alamy:** *Bildagentur Franz Waldhaeusl bl; Keith Levit c; ThinkStock br;* **Dreamstime.com:** *Alexandre Dvihally (tl); p100/101* **DK Images:** *Steve Gorton tcr; p102/103* **Alamy:** *Hortus b; D Hurst tcrB;* **Alamy:** *image100 tcr;* **DK Images:** *Geoff Brightling cAAr;* **Ingram Image Library:** *cAr; p104/105* **DK Images:** *Paul Bricknell cl(6); Jane Burton bcl; Geoff Dann cl(2); Max Gibbs cl(4); Frank Greenaway cl(3); Dave King cl(1), cAr; Tracy Morgan c(5); p106/107* **Alamy:** *Shotfile cr;* **DK Images:** *Geoff Brightling br; p110/111* **Alamy:** *RubberBall cr;* **DK Images:** *Andy Crawford cl; p112/113* **Alamy RF:** *BananaStock tcr; Image Source bl;* **DK Images:** *cl;* **Ingram Image Library:** *bcrA; p114/115* **Alamy:** *FogStock tcr;* **Alamy:** *Image Source cAr; Index Stock cAl; p116/117* **Alamy:** *image100 cAl; p118/119* **Alamy RF:** *Pixland tcr;* **GettyNews:** *Giuseppe Cacace c; p120/121* **Alamy:** *ImageState / Pictor International cl;* **Alamy:** *Sarkis Images tcr;* **DK Images:** *cBl, bcl; p122/123* **Alamy:** *BananaStock cA;* **Ingram Image Library:** *cl; p124/125* **Alamy:** *ImageState / Pictor International bclA;* **DK Images:** *cBl, bcl; Paul Bricknell tc(5); Geoff Dann tc(3); Max Gibbs tc(1); Frank Greenaway tc(2); Dave King tc(4); Tracy Morgan tc(6); p126/127* **Alamy:** *Image Farm Inc bl; p128* **DK Images:** *Neil Mersh.*

All other images **Mike Good.**